Joan of Arc

Ronald Sutherland Gower

Contents

DEDICATION. 7
PREFACE. 8
CHAPTER I. THE CALL. *9*
CHAPTER II. THE DELIVERY OF ORLEANS. *32*
CHAPTER III. THE CORONATION AT RHEIMS. *50*
CHAPTER IV. THE CAPTURE. *68*
CHAPTER V. IMPRISONMENT AND TRIAL *86*
CHAPTER VI. MARTYRDOM. 152
CHAPTER VII. THE REHABILITATION. 159

JOAN OF ARC

BY

Ronald Sutherland Gower

DEDICATION.

My mother had what the French call a *culte* for the heroine whose life I have attempted to write in the following pages.

It was but natural that one who loved and admired all that is good and beautiful and high-minded should have a strong feeling of admiration for the memory of Joan of Arc. On the pedestal of the bronze statue, which my mother placed in her house at Cliveden, are inscribed those words which sum up the life and career of the Maid of Orleans:--

'La grande pitié qu'il y avait au royaume de France.'

Thinking that could my mother have read the following pages she would have approved the feeling which prompted me to write them, I inscribe this little book to her beloved memory.

R.G.
ARCACHON,
November 29.

PREFACE.

The authors whose works I have chiefly used in writing this Life of Joan of Arc, are--first, Quicherat, who was the first to publish at length the Minutes of the two trials concerning the Maid--that of her trial at Rouen in 1430, and of her rehabilitation in 1456, and who unearthed so many chronicles relating to her times; secondly, Wallon, whose Life of Joan of Arc is of all the fullest and most reliable; thirdly, Fabre, who has within the last few years published several most important books respecting the life and death of Joan. Fabre was the first to make a translation in full of the two trials which Quicherat had first published in the original Latin text.

Thinking references at the foot of the page a nuisance to the reader, these have been avoided.

R.G.
LONDON,
January, 1893.

CHAPTER I.
THE CALL.

Never perhaps in modern times had a country sunk so low as France, when, in the year 1420, the treaty of Troyes was signed. Henry V. of England had made himself master of nearly the whole kingdom; and although the treaty only conferred the title of Regent of France on the English sovereign during the lifetime of the imbecile Charles VI., Henry was assured in the near future of the full possession of the French throne, to the exclusion of the Dauphin. Henry received with the daughter of Charles VI. the Duchy of Normandy, besides the places conquered by Edward III. and his famous son; and of fourteen provinces left by Charles V. to his successor only three remained in the power of the French crown. The French Parliament assented to these hard conditions, and but one voice was raised in protest to the dismemberment of France; that solitary voice, a voice crying in a wilderness, was that of Charles the Dauphin-- afterwards Charles VII. Henry V. had fondly imagined that by the treaty of Troyes and his marriage with a French princess the war, which had lasted over a century between the two countries, would now cease, and that France would lie for ever at the foot of England. Indeed, up to Henry's death, at the end of August 1422, events seemed to justify such hopes; but after a score of years from Henry's death France had recovered almost the whole of her lost territory.

There is nothing in history more strange and yet more true than the story which has been told so often, but which never palls in its interest--that life of the maiden through whose instrumentality France regained her place among the nations. No poet's fancy has spun from out his imagination a more glorious tale, or pictured in glowing words an epic of heroic love and transcendent valour, to compete with the actual reality of the career of this simple village maiden of old France: she who, almost unassisted and alone, through her intense love of her native land and deep pity for the woes of her people, was enabled, when the day of action at length arrived, to triumph over unnumbered obstacles, and, in spite of all opposition, ridicule, and contumely, to fulfil her glorious mission.

Sainte-Beuve has written that, in his opinion, the way to honour the history of Joan of Arc is to tell the truth about her as simply as possible. This has been my object in the following pages.

On the border of Lorraine and Champagne, in the canton of the Barrois--between the rivers Marne and Meuse--extended, at the time of which we are writing, a vast forest, called the Der. By the side of a little streamlet, which took its source from the river Meuse, and dividing it east by west, stands the village of Domremy. The southern portion, confined within its banks and watered by its stream, contained a little fortalice, with a score of cottages grouped around. These were situated in the county of Champagne, under the suzerainty of the Count de Bar.

The northern side of the village, containing the church, belonged to the Manor of Vaucouleurs. In this part of the village, in a cottage built between the church and the rivulet close by, Joan of Arc was born, on or about the 6th of January, 1412. The house which now exists on the site of her birthplace was built in 1481, but the little streamlet still takes its course at its foot. Michelet, in his account of the heroine, says the station in life of Joan's father was that of a labourer; later investigations have proved that he was what we should call a small farmer. In the course of the trial held for the rehabilitation of Joan of Arc's memory, which yields valuable and authentic information relating to her family as well as to her life and actions, it appears that the neighbours of the heroine deposed that her parents were well-to-do agriculturists, holding a small property besides this house at Domremy; they held about twenty acres of land, twelve of which were arable, four meadow-land, and four for fuel. Besides this they had some two to three hundred francs kept safe in case of emergency, and the furniture goods and chattels of their modest home. The money thus kept in case of sudden trouble came in usefully when the family had to escape from the English to Neufchateau. All told, the fortune of the family of Joan attained an annual income of about two hundred pounds of our money, a not inconsiderable revenue at that time; and with it they were enabled to raise a family in comfort, and to give alms and hospitality to the poor, and wandering friars and other needy wayfarers, then so common in the land.

Two documents lately discovered prove Joan's father to have held a position of some importance at Domremy. In the one, dated 1423, he is styled 'doyen' (senior inhabitant) of the village, which gave him rank next to the Mayor. In the other, four years later, he fills a post which tallies with what is called in Scotland the Procurator-fiscal.

The name of the family was Arc, and much ink has been shed as to the origin of that name. By some it is derived from the village of d'Arc, in the Barrois, now in the department of the Haute Marne; and this hypothesis is as good as any other.

Jacques d'Arc had taken to wife one Isabeau Romee, from the village of Vouthon, near Domremy. Isabeau is said to have had some property in her native village. The family of Jacques d'Arc and Isabella or Isabeau consisted of five children: three sons, Jacquemin, Jean, and Pierre, and two daughters, the elder Catherine, the younger Jeanne, or Jennette, as she was generally called in her family, whose name was to go through the ages as one of the most glorious in any land.

Well favoured by nature was the birthplace of Joan of Arc, with its woods of chestnut and of oak, then in their primeval abundance. The vine of Greux, which was famous all over the country-side as far back as the fourteenth century, grew on the southern slopes of the hills about Joan's birthplace. Beneath these vineyards the fields were thickly clothed with rye and oats, and the meadow-lands washed by the waters of the Meuse were fragrant with hay that had no rival in the country. It was in these rich fields that, after the hay-making was over, the peasants let out their cattle to graze, the number of each man's kine corresponding with the number of fields which he owned and which he had reaped.

The little maid sometimes helped her father's labourers, and the idea has become general that Joan of Arc was a shepherdess; in reality, it was only an occasional occupation, and probably undertaken by Joan out of mere good-nature, seeing that her parents were well-to-do people. All that we gather of Joan's early years proves her nature to have been a compound of love and goodness. Every trait recorded of the little maid's life at home which has come down to us reveals a mixture of amiability, unselfishness, and charity. From her earliest years she loved to help the weak and poor: she was known, when there was no room for the weary wayfarer to pass the night in her parents' house, to give up her bed to them, and to sleep on the floor, by the hearth.

She loved her mother tenderly, and in her trial she bore witness before men to the good influence that she had derived from that parent. Isabeau d'Arc appears to have been a devout woman, and to have brought up her children to love work and religion. Joan loved to sit by her mother's side for the hour together, spinning, and doubtless listening to the stories of wars with the hereditary enemy. When she could be of use, Joan was ever ready to lend a hand to help her father or brothers in the rougher labours of coach-house, stable, or farmyard, to keep watch over the flocks as they browsed by the river-side along the meadow-lands.

Joan had not the defect of so many excellent but tedious women, who love talk for the mere sake of talking: she seems to have been reserved; but, as she proved later on, she was never at a loss for a word in season, and with a few words could speak volumes. From her childhood she showed an intense and ever-increasing devotion to things holy; her delight in prayer became almost a passion. She never wearied of visiting the churches in and about her native village, and she passed many an hour in a kind of rapt trance before the crucifixes and saintly images in these churches. Every morning saw her at her accustomed place at the early celebration of her Lord's Sacrifice; and if in the afternoon the evening bells sounded across the fields, she would kneel devoutly, and commune in her heart with her divine Master and adored saints. She loved above all things these evening bells, and, when it seemed to her the ringer grew negligent, would bribe him with some little gift--the worked wool from one of her sheep or some other trifle--to remind him in the future to be more instant in his office. That this little trait in Joan is true, we have the testimony of the bell-ringer himself to attest.

This devotion to her religious duties had not the effect of making Joan less of a companion to her fellow-villagers. She could not have been so much beloved by them as she was had she held herself aloof from them: on the contrary, Joan enjoyed to play with the lads and village lasses; and we hear of her swiftness of foot in the race, of her gracefulness in the village dance, either by the stream or around an old oak-tree in the forest, which was said to be the favourite haunt of the fairies.

Often in the midst of these sports Joan would break away from her companions, and enter some church or chapel, where she placed garlands of flowers around statues of her beloved saints.

Thus passed away the early years of the maiden's gentle life, among her native fields, with nothing especially to distinguish her from her companions beyond her goodness and piety. A great change, however, was near at hand. The first of those mysterious and supernatural events which played so all-important a part in the life of our heroine occurred in the summer of 1425, when Joan was in her thirteenth year. In her trial at Rouen, on being asked by her judges what was the first manifestation of these visions, she answered that the first indication of what she always called 'My voices' was that of St. Michel. It is not a little remarkable that this vision of St. Michel, the patron saint of the French army, should have taken place in the summer of 1425, at the time of a double defeat by land and sea of the enemy of France, and when the Holy Mount in Normandy, crowned by the chapel guarded by St. Michel, was once again in the hands of the French. At the same time, Joan of Arc experienced some of the hardships of war when the country around Domremy was overrun by the enemy; and the little household of the Arcs had to fly for shelter to the neighbouring village of Chateauneuf, in Lorraine.

I will pass somewhat rapidly over the visions, or rather revelations--for, whatever doubts one may hold as to such heavenly messengers appearing literally on this earth, no man can honestly doubt that Joan believed as firmly in these unearthly visitants coming from Heaven direct as she did in the existence of herself or of her parents. On the subject of these voices and visions no one has written with more sense than a distinguished prelate who was a contemporary of the heroine's--namely, Thomas Basin, Bishop of Lisieux, who, in a work relating to Joan of Arc, writes thus:--

'As regards her mission, and as regards the apparitions and revelations that she affirmed having had, we leave to every one the liberty to believe as he pleases, to reject or to hold, according to his point of view or way of thinking. What is important regarding these visions is the fact that Joan had herself no shadow of a doubt regarding their reality, and it was their effect upon her, and not her natural inclination, which impelled her to leave her parents and her home to undertake great perils and to endure great hardships, and, as it proved, a terrible death. It was these visions and voices, and they alone, which made her believe that she would succeed, if she obeyed them, in saving her country and in replacing her king on his throne. It was these visions and voices which finally enabled her to do those marvellous deeds, and accomplish what appeared to all the world the impossible; these voices and visions will ever be connected with Joan of Arc, and with her deathless fame and glory.'

From the year 1425 till 1428, the apparitions and voices were heard and seen more or less frequently.

It is the year 1427: all that remains to Charles of his kingdom north of the Loire, with the exception of Tournay, are a pitiful half-dozen places. Among these is Vaucouleurs, near Domremy. They are defended by a body of men under the command of a knight, Robert de Baudricourt, who is about to play an important part in the history of Joan.

In one of her visions the maid was told to seek this knight, that through his help she might be brought to the French Court; for the voices had told her she might find the King and tell him her message, by which she should deliver the land from the English, and restore him to his throne. There had not been wanting legends and prophecies upon the country-side which may have impressed Joan, and helped her to believe that it was her mission to deliver France. One of the prophecies was to the effect that a maiden from the borders of Lorraine should save France, that this maiden would appear from a place near an oak forest. This seemed to point directly to our heroine. The old oak-tree haunted by the fairies, the neighbouring country of Lorraine, were all in help of the tradition. Since the betrayal of her husband's country by the wife of Charles VI., another saying had been spread abroad throughout all that remained of that small portion of France still held by the French King--namely, that although France would be lost by a woman, a maiden should save it. Any hope to the people in those distressful days was eagerly seized on; and although the first prophecy dated from the mythical times of Merlin, it stirred the people, especially when, later on, Joan of Arc appeared among them, and her story became known.

These prophecies appear to have struck deeply into Joan's soul; they, and her voices aiding, made her believe she was the maiden by whom her country would be delivered from the presence of the enemy. But how was she to make her parents understand that it was their child who was appointed by Heaven to fulfil this great deliverance? Her father seems to have been a somewhat harsh, at any rate a practical, parent. When told of her intention to join the army, he said he would rather throw her into the river than allow her to do so. An attempt was made by her parents to induce her to marry. They tried their best, but Joan would none of it; and bringing the case before the lawyers at Toul, where she proved that she had never thought of marrying a youth whom her parents required her to wed, she gained her cause and her freedom.

In order to take the first step in her mission, Joan felt it necessary to rely on some one outside her immediate family. A distant relation of her mother's, one Durand Laxart, who with his wife lived in a little village then named Burey-le-Petit (now called Burey-en-Vaux), near Vaucouleurs, was the relation in whose care she placed her fate. With him and his wife Joan remained eight days; and it might have been then that the plan was arranged to hold an interview with Baudricourt at Vaucouleurs, in order to see whether that knight would interest himself in Joan's mission.

The interview took place about the middle of the month of May (1428), and nothing could have been less propitious. A soldier named Bertrand de Poulangy, who was one of the garrison of Vaucouleurs, was an eye-witness of the meeting. He accompanied Joan of Arc later on to Chinon, and left a record of the almost brutal manner with which Baudricourt received the Maid. From this soldier's narrative we possess one of the rare glimpses which have come down to us of the appearance of the heroine: not indeed a description of what would be of such intense interest as to make known to us the appearance and features of her face; but he describes her dress, which was that then worn by the better-to-do agricultural class of Lorraine peasant women, made of rough red serge, the cap such as is still worn by the peasantry of her native place.

It is much to be regretted that no portrait of Joan of Arc exists either in sculpture or painting. A life-size bronze statue which portrayed the Maid kneeling on one side of a crucifix, with Charles VII. opposite, forming part of a group near the old bridge of Orleans, was destroyed by the Huguenots; and all the portraits of Joan painted in oils are spurious. None are earlier than the sixteenth century, and all are mere imaginary daubs. In most of these Joan figures in a hat and feathers, of the style worn in the Court of Francis I. From various contemporary notices, it appears that her hair was dark in colour, as in Bastien Lepage's celebrated picture, which supplies as good an idea of what Joan may have been as any pictured representation of her form and face. Would that the frescoes which Montaigne describes as being painted on the front of the house upon the site of which Joan was born could have come down to us. They might have given some conception of her appearance. Montaigne saw those frescoes on his way to Italy, and says that all the front of the house was painted with representations of her deeds, but even in his day they were much injured.

When Joan at length stood before the knight of Vaucouleurs, she told him boldly that she had come to him by God's command, and that she was destined to give the King victory over the English. She even said that she was assured that early in the following March this would be accomplished, and that the Dauphin would then be crowned at Rheims, for all these things had been promised to her through her Lord.

'And who is he?' asked de Baudricourt.

'He is the King of Heaven,' she answered.

The knight treated Joan's words with derision, and Joan herself with insults; and thus ended the first of their interviews.

It was only in the season of Lent of the next year (March 1427) that Joan again sought the aid of de Baudricourt. On the plea of attending her cousin Laxart's wife's confinement, Joan returned to Burey-le-Petit. She left Domremy without bidding her parents farewell; but it has been recorded by one of her friends, named Mengeth, a neighbour of the d'Arcs, that she told this woman of her intention of going to Vaucouleurs, and recommended her to God's keeping, as if she felt that she would not see her again. At Burey-le-Petit Joan remained between the end of January until her departure for Chinon, on the 23rd of February; and before taking final leave she asked and received her parents' pardon for her abrupt departure from them.

While with the Laxarts, news reached Vaucouleurs that the English had commenced the siege of Orleans. This intelligence brought matters to a crisis, for with the loss of Orleans the whole of what remained to the French King must fall into the hands of the enemy, and France felt her last hour of independence had come.

Joan determined on again seeking an interview with Robert de Baudricourt, and this second meeting between her and the knight, which took place six months after the first, had far happier results. As M. Simeon Luce has pointed out in his history of 'Jeanne d'Arc at Domremy,' the situation both of Charles VI. and of the knight of Vaucouleurs was far different in 1429 to what it had been when Joan first saw de Baudricourt at Vaucouleurs in the previous year. The most important stronghold held by the French in their ever-lessening territory was in utmost danger of falling into the grasp of the English; while de Baudricourt was anxiously waiting to hear whether his protector, the Duc de Bar, whom Bedford had summoned to enter into a treaty with the English, would not be prevailed upon to do so. If he consented, this would make the knight's tenure of Vaucouleurs impracticable. It was probably owing to this state of affairs that, on her second interview with the knight of Vaucouleurs, Joan of Arc was favourably received by him. Since the first visit to de Baudricourt by the Maid of Domremy, her name had become familiar to many of the people in and about Vaucouleurs. An officer named Jean de Metz has left some record of his meeting at this time with Joan; for he was afterwards examined among other witnesses at the time of the Maid's rehabilitation in 1456. De Metz describes the Maid as being clothed in a dress of coarse red serge, the same as she wore on her first visit to Vaucouleurs. When he questioned her as to what she expected to gain by coming again to Vaucouleurs, she answered that she had returned to induce Robert de Baudricourt to conduct her to the King; but that on her first visit he was deaf to her entreaties and prayers. But, she added, she was still determined to appear before Charles, even if she had to go to him all the way on her knees.

'For I alone,' she added, 'and no other person, whether he be King, or Duke, or daughter of the King of Scots' (alluding to the future wife of Charles VII.'s son, Louis XI.--Margaret of Scotland) 'can recover the kingdom of France.'

As far as her own wishes were concerned, she said she would prefer to return to her home, and to spin again by the side of her beloved mother; for, she added: 'I am not made to follow the career of a soldier; but I must go and carry out this my calling, for my Lord has appointed me to do so.'

'And who,' asked de Metz, 'is your Lord?'

'My Lord,' answered the Maid, 'is God Himself.'

The enthusiasm of Joan seems to have at once gained the soldier's heart. He took her by the hand, and swore that God willing he would accompany her to the King. When asked how soon she would be ready to start, she said that she was ready. 'Better to-day than to-morrow, and better to-morrow than later on.'

During her second visit to Vaucouleurs, Joan remained with the same friends as on her former visit; they appear to have been an honest couple, of the name of Le Royer. One day while Joan was helping in the domestic work of her hosts, and seated by the side of Catherine Le Royer, Robert de Baudricourt suddenly entered the room, accompanied by a priest, one Jean Fournier, in full canonicals. It appeared that the knight had conceived the brilliant idea of finding out, through the assistance of the holy man, whether Joan was under the influence of good or evil spirits, before allowing her to go to the King's Court.

As may be imagined, Joan received the priest with all respect, kneeling before him; and the good father was soon able to reassure de Baudricourt that the evil spirits had no part or parcel in the heart of the maid who received him with so much humility.

For three weeks Joan was left in suspense at Vaucouleurs, and probably it was not until a messenger had been sent to Chinon and had returned with a favourable answer, that at length de Baudricourt gave a somewhat unwilling consent to Joan's leaving Vaucouleurs on her mission to Chinon. During those weary weeks of anxious waiting, Joan's hostess bore witness in after days to the manner in which the time was passed: of how she would help Catherine in her spinning and other homely work, but, as when at home, her chief delight was to attend the Church services, and she would often remain to confession, after the early communion in the church. The chapel in which she worshipped was not the parochial church of Vaucouleurs, but was attached to the castle, and it still exists. In that castle chapel, and in a subterranean crypt beneath the Collegiate Church of Notre Dame de Vaucouleurs, Joan passed much of her time. Seven and twenty years after these events, one Jean le Fumeux, at that time a chorister of the chapel, a lad of eleven, bore witness, at the trial in which the memory of Joan was vindicated, to having often seen her kneeling before an image of the Virgin. This image, a battered and rude one, still exists. Nothing less artistic can be imagined; but no one, be his religious views what they may, be his abhorrence of Mariolatry as strong as that of a Calvinist, if he have a grain of sympathy in his nature for what is glorious in patriotism and sublime in devotion, can look on that battered and broken figure without a feeling deeper than one of ordinary curiosity.

A short time before leaving Vaucouleurs, Joan made a visit into Lorraine--a visit which proved how early her fame had spread abroad. The then reigning Duke of that province, Charles II. of Lorraine, an aged and superstitious prince, had heard of the mystic Maid of Domremy, and he had expressed his wish to see her, probably thinking that she might afford him relief from the infirmities from which he suffered. Whatever the reason may have been, he sent her an urgent request to visit him, a message with which Joan at once complied.

Accompanied by Jean de Metz, Joan went to Toul, and thence with her cousin, Durand Laxart, she proceeded to Nancy. Little is known of her deeds while there. She visited Duke Charles, and gave him some advice as to how he should regain his character more than his health, over which she said she had no control. The old Duke appears to have been rather a reprobate, but whether he profited by Joan's advice does not appear.

Possibly this rather vague visit of the Maid's to Nancy was undertaken as a kind of test as to how she would comport herself among dukes and princes. That she showed most perfect modesty of bearing under somewhat difficult circumstances seems to have struck those who were with her at Nancy. She also showed practical sagacity; for she advised Duke Charles to give active support to the French King, and persuaded him to allow his son-in-law, young Rene of Anjou, Duke of Bar, to enter the ranks of the King's army, and even to allow him to accompany her to the Court at Chinon. By this she bound the more than lukewarm Duke of Lorraine to exert all his influence on the side of King Charles.

Before leaving Nancy on her return to Vaucouleurs, Joan visited a famous shrine, not far from the capital, dedicated to St. Nicolas, after which she hastened back to Vaucouleurs to make ready for an immediate start for Chinon.

Joan's equipment for her journey to Chinon was subscribed for by the people of Vaucouleurs; for among the common folk there, as wherever she was known, her popularity was great. She seems to have won in every instance the hearts of the good simple peasantry, the poorer classes in general, called by a saintly King of France the 'common people of our Lord,' who believed in her long before others of the higher classes and the patricians were persuaded to put any faith in her. To the peasantry Joan was already the maiden pointed out in the old prophecy then known all over France, which said that the country would be first lost by a woman and then recovered by a maiden hailing from Lorraine. The former was believed to be the Queen-mother, who had sided with the English; Joan, the Maid out of Lorraine who should save France, and by whose arm the English would be driven out of the country.

Clad in a semi-male attire, composed of a tight-fitting doublet of dark cloth and tunic reaching to the knees, high leggings and spurred boots, with a black cap on her head, and a hauberk, the Maid was armed with lance and sword, the latter the gift of de Baudricourt. Her good friends of Vaucouleurs had also subscribed for a horse. Thus completely equipped, she prepared for war, ready for her eventful voyage. Her escort consisted of a knight named Colet de Vienne, accompanied by his squire, one Richard l'Archer, two men-at-arms from Vaucouleurs, and the two knights Bertrand de Poulangy and Jean de Metz--eight men in all, well armed and well mounted, and thoroughly prepared to defend their charge should the occasion arise. Nor were precautions and means of repelling an attack unnecessary, for at this time the country around Vaucouleurs was infested by roving bands of soldiers belonging to the Anglo-Burgundian party. Especially dangerous was that stretch of country lying between Vaucouleurs and Joinville, the first of the many stages on the way to Chinon. Although the knights and men of the small expedition were not without apprehension, Joan seems to have shown no sign of fear: calm and cheerful, she said that, being under the protection of Heaven, they had nothing to fear, for that no evil could befall her.

There still exists the narrow gate of the old castle of Vaucouleurs through which that little band rode out into the night; hard by is the small subterranean chapel, now under repair, where Joan had passed so many hours of her weary weeks of waiting at Vaucouleurs. The old gate is still called the French Gate, as it was in the days of the Maid.

It was the evening of the 23rd of February, 1429, that the little band rode away into the open country on their perilous journey. Joan, besides adopting a military attire, had trimmed her dark hair close, as it was then the fashion of knights to do-- cut round above the ears. Even this harmless act was later brought as an accusation against her. Joan was then in her seventeenth year, and, although nothing but tradition has reached us of her looks and outward form, it is not difficult to imagine her as she rides out of that old gate, a comely maid, with a frank, brave countenance, lit up by the flame of an intense enthusiasm for her country and people. There can be no doubt that by her companions in arms--rough soldiers though most of them were--she was held in veneration; they bore testimony to their feelings by a kind of adoration for one who seemed indeed to them more than mortal. Wherever Joan appeared, this feeling of veneration spread rapidly through the length and breadth of the land; and the people were wont to speak of the future saviour of France, not by the name of Joan the Maid, or Joan of Arc, but as the Angelic One--'l'Angelique.'

Among the crowd who gathered to see Joan depart was de Baudricourt, who then made amends for his rudeness and churlish behaviour on her first visit by presenting her with his own sword, and bidding her heartily god-speed. 'Advienne que pourra!' was his parting salute.

The journey between Vaucouleurs and Chinon occupied eleven days. Not only was the danger of attack from the English and Burgundian soldiers a great and a constant one, but the winter, which had been exceptionally wet, had flooded all the rivers. Five of these had to be crossed--namely, the Marne, the Aube, the Seine, the Yonne, and the Loire: and most of the bridges and fords of these rivers were strictly guarded by the enemy. The little band, for greater security, mostly travelled during the night. Their first halt was made at the Monastery of Saint-Urbain-les-Joinville. The Celibat of this monastery was named Arnoult d'Aunoy, and was a relative of de Baudricourt. After leaving that shelter they had to camp out in the open country.

Joan's chief anxiety was that she might be able to attend Mass every day. 'If we are able to attend the service of the Church, all will be well,' she said to her escort. The soldiers only twice allowed her the opportunity of doing so, on one occasion in the principal church of the town of Auxerre.

They crossed the Loire at Gien; and at that place, in the church dedicated to one of Joan's special saints--St. Catherine, for whom she held a personal adoration--she thrice attended Mass.

When the little band entered Touraine, they were out of danger, and here the news of the approach of the Maid spread like wildfire over the country-side. Even the besieged burghers of Orleans learned that the time of their delivery from the English was at hand.

Perhaps it was when passing through Fierbois that Joan may have been told of the existence in its church of the sword which so conspicuously figured in her later story, and was believed to have been miraculously revealed to her.

A letter was despatched from Fierbois to Charles at Chinon, announcing the

Maid's approach, and craving an audience. At length, on the 6th of March, Joan of Arc arrived beneath the long stretch of castle walls of the splendid old Castle of Chinon.

That imposing ruin on the banks of the river Vienne is even in its present abandoned state one of the grandest piles of mediaeval building in the whole of France. Crowning the rich vale of Touraine, with the river winding below, and reflecting its castle towers in the still water, this time-honoured home of our Plantagenet kings has been not inaptly compared to Windsor. Beneath the castle walls and the river, nestles the quaint old town, in which are mediaeval houses once inhabited by the court and followers of the French and English kings.

When Joan arrived at Chinon, Charles's affairs were in a very perilous state. The yet uncrowned King of France regarded the chances of being able to hold his own in France as highly problematical. He had doubts as to his legitimacy. Financially, so low were his affairs that even the turnspits in the palace were clamouring for their unpaid wages. The unfortunate monarch had already sold his jewels and precious trinkets. Even his clothes showed signs of poverty and patching, and to such a state of penury was he reduced that his bootmaker, finding that the King was unable to pay him the price of a new pair of boots, and not trusting the royal credit, refused to leave the new boots, and Charles had to wear out his old shoe-leather. All that remained in the way of money in the royal chest consisted of four gold 'ecus.' To such a pitch of distress had the poor King, who was contemptuously called by the English the King of Bourges, sunken.

Now that Orleans was in daily peril of falling into the hands of the English, and with Paris and Rouen in their hold, the wretched sovereign had serious thoughts of leaving his ever-narrowing territory and taking refuge either in Spain or in Scotland. Up to this time in his life Charles had shown little strength of character. His existence was passed among a set of idle courtiers. He had placed himself and his broken fortunes in the hands of the ambitious La Tremoille, whose object it was that the King should be a mere cipher in his hands, and who lulled him into a false security by encouraging him to continue a listless career of self-indulgence in his various palaces and pleasure castles on the banks of the Loire. Charles had, indeed, become a mere tool in the hands of this powerful minister. The historian Quicherat has summed up George de la Tremoille's character as an avaricious courtier, false and despotic, with sufficient talent to make a name and a fortune by being a traitor to every side. That such a man did not see Joan of Arc's arrival with a favourable eye is not a matter of surprise, and La Tremoille seems early to have done his utmost to undermine the Maid's influence with his sovereign. From the day she arrived at Chinon, if not even before her arrival there--if we may trust one story--an ambush was arranged by Tremoille to cut her off with her escort. That plot failed, but her capture at Compiegne may be indirectly traced to La Tremoille's machinations.

Those who have visited Chinon will recall the ancient and picturesque street, named La Haute Rue Saint Maurice, which runs beneath and parallel with the castle walls and the Vienne. Local tradition pointed out till very recently, in this old street, the stone well on the side of which the Maid of Domremy placed her foot on her arrival in the town. This ancient well stone has recently been removed by the Municipality of Chinon, but fortunately the 'Margelle' (to use the native term) has come into reverent hands, and the stone, with its deeply dented border, reminding one of the artistic wells in Venice, is religiously preserved.

Of Chinon it has been said:

Chynon, petit ville,
Grande renom.

Its renown dates back from the early days of our Plantagenets, when they lived in the old fortress above its dwellings: how Henry III. died of a broken heart, and the fame of Rabelais, will ever be associated with the ancient castle and town. Still, the deathless interest of Chinon is owing to the residence of the Maid of Domremy--as one has a better right to call her than of Orleans--in those early days of her short career, in its burgh and castle. In or near the street La Haute Rue Saint Maurice, hard by a square which now bears the name of the heroine, Joan of Arc arrived at noon on Sunday, the 6th of March.

It would be interesting to know in which of the old gabled houses Joan resided during the two days before she was admitted to enter the castle. Local tradition reports that she dwelt with a good housewife ('chez une bonne femme'). According to a contemporary plan of Chinon, dated 1430, a house which belonged to a family named La Barre was where she lodged; and although the actual house of the La

Barres cannot be identified, there are many houses in the street of Saint Maurice old enough to have witnessed the advent of the Maid on that memorable Sunday in the month of March 1430. Few French towns are so rich in the domestic architecture of the better kind dating from the early part of the fifteenth century as that of Chinon; and now that Rouen, Orleans, and Poitiers have been so terribly modernised, a journey to Chinon well repays the trouble. Little imagination is required to picture the street with its crowd of courtiers and Court hangers-on, upon their way to and from the castle above; so mercifully have time and that far greater destroyer of things of yore dealt with this old thoroughfare.

Two days elapsed before Joan was admitted to the presence of the King. A council had been summoned in the castle to determine whether the Maid should be received by the monarch. The testimony of the knights who had accompanied the Maid from Vaucouleurs carried the day in her favour.

While waiting to see the King, we have from Joan's own lips a description of how her time was passed. 'I was constantly at prayers in order that God should send the King a sign. I was lodging with a good woman when that sign was given him, and then I was summoned to the King.'

The church in which she passed her time in prayer was doubtless that of Saint Maurice, close by the place at which she lodged. It owed its origin to Henry II. of England; it is a rare and beautiful little building of good Norman architecture, but much defaced by modern restoration. Its age is marked by the depth at which its pavement stands, the ground rising many feet above its present level.

A reliable account of Joan of Arc's interview with King Charles has come down to us, as have so many other facts in her life's history, through the witnesses examined at the time of the heroine's rehabilitation. Foremost among these is the testimony of a priest named Pasquerel, who was soon to become Joan's almoner, and to accompany her in her warfare. He tells how, when Joan was on her road to enter the castle, a soldier used some coarse language as he saw the young Maid pass by--some rude remark which the fellow qualified with an oath. Turning to him, the Maid rebuked him for blaspheming, and added that he had denied his God at the very moment in which he would be summoned before his Judge, for that within an hour he would appear before the heavenly throne. The soldier was drowned within the hour. At least such is the tale as told by Priest Pasquerel.

The castle was shrouded in outer darkness, but brilliantly lit within, as Joan entered its gates. The King's Chamberlain, the Comte de Vendome, received the Maid at the entrance of the royal apartments, and ushered her into the great gallery, of which fragments still exist--a blasted fireplace, and sufficient remains of the original stone-work to prove that this hall was the principal apartment in the palace. Flambeaux and torches glowed from the roof and from the sides of this hall, and here the Court had assembled, half amused, half serious, as to the arrival of the peasant girl, about whom there had been so much strange gossip stirring. Now the grass grows in wild luxuriance over the pavement, and the ivy clings to the old walls of that noble room, in which, perhaps, the most noteworthy of all recorded meetings between king and subject then took place. A score of torches held by pages lit the sides of the chamber. Before these were ranged the knights and ladies, the latter clothed in the fantastically rich costume of that time, with high erections on their heads, from which floated long festoons of cloth, and glittering with the emblems of their families on their storied robes. The King, in order to test the divination of the Maid, had purposely clad himself in common garb, and had withdrawn himself behind his more brilliantly attired courtiers.

Ascending the flight of eighteen steps which led into the hall, and following Vendome, Joan passed across the threshold of the hall, and, without a moment's hesitation singling out the King at the end of the gallery, walked to within a few paces of him, and falling on her knees before him--'the length of a lance,' as one of the spectators recorded--said, 'God give you good life, noble King!' ('Dieu vous donne bonne vie, gentil Roi').

'But,' said Charles, 'I am not the King. This,' pointing to one of his courtiers, 'is the King.'

Joan, however, was not to be hoodwinked, and, finding that in spite of his subterfuges he was known, Charles acknowledged his identity, and entered at once with Joan on the subject of her mission.

It appears, from all the accounts which have come to us of this interview, that Charles was at first somewhat loth to take Joan and her mission seriously. He appears to have treated the Maid as a mere visionary; but after an interview which the King gave her apart from the crowded gallery, when she is supposed to have revealed to him a secret known only to himself, his whole manner changed, and from that moment Joan exercised a strong influence over the man, all-vacillating as was his character. It has never been known what words actually passed in this private interview between the pair, but the subject probably was connected with a doubt that had long tortured the mind of the King--namely, whether he were legitimately the heir to the late King's throne. At any rate the impression Joan had produced on the King was, after that conversation, a favourable one, and Charles commanded that, instead of returning to her lodging in the town, Joan should be lodged in the castle.

The tower which she occupied still exists--one of the large circular towers on the third line of the fortifications. A gloomy-looking cryptal room on the ground floor was probably the one occupied by Joan. It goes by the name of Belier's Tower--a knight whose wife, Anne de Maille, bore a reputation for great goodness among the people of the Court. Close to Belier's Tower is a chapel within another part of the castle grounds, but the church which in those days stood hard by Joan's tower has long since disappeared--its site is now a mass of wild foliage.

While Joan was at Chinon, there arrived, from his three years' imprisonment in England, the young Duke of Anjou. Of all those who were attached to the Court and related to the French sovereign, this young Prince was the most sympathetic to Joan of Arc. He seems to have fulfilled the character of some hero of romance more than any of the French princes of that time, and Joan at once found in him a chivalrous ally and a firm friend. That she admired him we cannot doubt, and she loved to call him her knight.

Hurrying to Chinon, having heard of the Maid of Domremy's arrival, he found Joan with the King. Her enthusiasm was contagious with the young Prince, who declared how eagerly he would help her in her enterprise.

'The more there are of the blood royal of France to help in our enterprise the better,' answered Joan.

Many obstacles had still to be met before the King accorded liberty of action to the Maid. La Tremoille and others of his stamp threw all the difficulties they could suggest in the way of Joan of Arc's expedition to deliver Orleans: these men preferred their easy life at Chinon to the arbitrament of battle. In vain Joan sought the King and pressed him to come to a decision: one day he said he would consent to her progress, and the following he refused to give his consent. He listened to the

Maid, but also to the courtiers, priests, and lawyers, and among so many counsellors he could come to no determination.

Joan during these days trained herself to the vocation which her career compelled her to follow. We hear of her on one occasion surprising the King and the Court by the dexterity with which she rode and tilted with a lance. From the young Duke of Alencon she received the gift of a horse; and the King carried out on a large scale what de Baudricourt had done on a small one, by making her a gift of arms and accoutrements. Before, however, deciding to entrust the fate of hostilities into the hands of the Maid, it was decided that the advice and counsel of the prelates assembled at Poitiers should be taken.

It was in the Great Hall of that town that the French Parliament held its conferences. The moment was critical, for should the decision of these churchmen be favourable to Joan, then Charles could no longer have any scruples in making use of her abilities, and of profiting by her influence.

It was, therefore, determined that Joan should be examined by the Parliament and clergy assembled at Poitiers. The King in person accompanied the Maid to the Parliament. The majestic hall, which still calls forth the admiration of all travellers at Poitiers, is little changed in its appearance since the time of that memorable event. It is one of the noblest specimens of domestic architecture in France: its graceful pillars and arched roof, and immense fireplace, remain as they were in the early days of the fifteenth century.

Of the proceedings of that examination unfortunately no complete report exists. Within a tower connected with the Parliament Hall is still pointed out a little chamber, said to have been occupied by the Maid while undergoing this, the first of her judicial and clerical examinations. But later investigations point to her having been lodged in a house within the town belonging to the family of the Parliamentary Advocate-General, Maitre Jean Rabuteau.

It must have been a solemn moment for Joan when summoned for the first time into the presence of the Court of bishops, judges, and lawyers, whom Charles had gathered together to examine her on her visions and on her mission. The orders had been sent out by the King and the Archbishop of Rheims; Gerard Machot, the Bishop of Castres and the King's confessor; Simon Bonnet, afterwards Bishop of Senlis; and the Bishops of Macquelonne and of Poitiers. Among the lesser dignitaries of the Church was present a Dominican monk, named Sequier, whose account of the proceedings, and the notes kept by Gobert Thibault, an equerry of the King, are the only records of the examination extant. The scantiness of these accounts is all the more to be regretted, inasmuch as Joan frequently referred to the questions made to her, and her answers, at this trial at Poitiers, during her trial at Rouen; and they would probably have thrown much light on the obscure passages of her early years, for at Poitiers she had not to guard against hostile inquisition, and, doubtless, gave her questioners a full and free record of her past life.

The first conference between these prelates, lawyers, and Joan lasted two hours. At first they appeared to doubt the Maid, but her frank and straightforward answers to all the questions put her impressed them with the truth of her character. They were, according to the old chronicles, 'grandement ebahis comme une ce simple bergere jeune fille pouvait ainsi repondre.'

One of her examiners, Jean Lombard by name, a professor of theology from the University of Paris, in asking Joan what had induced her to visit the King, was told she had been encouraged so to do by 'her voices'--those voices which had taught her the great pity felt by her for the land of France; that although at first she had hesitated to obey them, they became ever more urgent, and commanded her to go.

'And, Joan,' then asked a doctor of theology named William Aymeri, 'why do you require soldiers, if you tell us that it is God's will that the English shall be driven out of France? If that is the case, then there is no need of soldiers, for surely, if it be God's will that the enemy should fly the country, go they must!'

To which Joan answered: 'The soldiers will do the fighting, and God will give the victory!'

Sequier, whose account of the proceedings has come down to us, then asked Joan in what language the Saints addressed her.

'In a better one than yours,' she answered.

Now Brother Sequier, although a doctor of theology, had a strong and disagreeable accent which he had brought from his native town of Limoges, and, doubtless, the other clerks and priests tittered not a little at Joan's answer. Sequier appears to have been somewhat irritated, and sharply asked Joan whether she believed in God.

'Better than you do,' was the reply; but Sequier, who is described as a 'bien aigre homme,' was not yet satisfied, and returned to the charge. Like the Pharisees, he wished for a sign, and he declared that he for one could not believe in the sacred mission of the Maid, did she not show them all a sign, nor without such a sign could he advise the King to place any one in peril, merely on the strength of Joan's declaration and word.

To this Joan said that she had not come to Poitiers to show signs, but she added:--

'Let me go to Orleans, and there you will be able to judge by the signs I shall show wherefore I have been sent on this mission. Let the force of soldiers with me be as small as you choose; but to Orleans I must go!'

For three weeks did these conferences last. Nothing was neglected to discover every detail regarding Joan's life: of her childhood, of her family and her friends. And one of the Council visited Domremy to ferret out all the details that could be got at. Needless to say, all that he heard only redounded to the Maid's credit; nothing transpired which was not honourable to the Maid's character and way of life, and in keeping with the testimony Jean de Metz and Poulangy had given the King at Chinon.

One day she said to one of the Council, Pierre de Versailles, 'I believe you have come to put questions to me, and although I know not A or B, what I do know is that I am sent by the King of Heaven to raise the siege of Orleans, and to conduct the King to Rheims, in order that he shall be there anointed and crowned.'

On another occasion she addressed the following words in a letter which John Erault took down from her dictation--to write she knew not--to the English commanders before Orleans: 'In the name of the King of Heaven I command you, Suffolk [spelt in the missive Suffort], Scales [Classidas], and Pole [La Poule], to return to England.'

One sees by the above missive that the French spelling of English names was about as correct in the fifteenth as it is in the nineteenth century.

What stirred the curiosity of Joan's examiners was to try and discover whether her reported visions and her voices were from Heaven or not. This was the crucial question over which these churchmen and lawyers puzzled their brains during those three weeks of the blithe spring-tide at Poitiers. How were they to arrive at a certain knowledge regarding those mystic portents? All the armoury of theological knowledge accumulated by the doctors of the Church was made use of; but this availed less than the simple answers of Joan in bringing conviction to these puzzled pundits that her call was a heavenly one. When they produced piles of theological books and parchments, Joan simply said: 'God's books are to me more than all these.'

When at length it was officially notified that the Parliament approved and sanctioned the mission of the Maid, and that nothing against her had appeared which could in any way detract from the faith she professed to follow out her mission of deliverance, the rejoicing in the good town of Poitiers was extreme. The glad news spread rapidly over the country, and fluttered the hearts of the besieged within the walls of Orleans. The cry was, 'When will the angelic one arrive?' The brave Dunois--Bastard of Orleans--in command of the French in that city, had ere this sent two knights, Villars and Jamet de Tilloy, to hear all details about the Maid, whose advent was so eagerly looked forward to. These messengers of Dunois had seen and spoken with Joan, and on their return to Orleans Dunois allowed them to tell the citizens their impressions of the Maid. Those people at Orleans were now as enthusiastic about the deliverance as the inhabitants at Poitiers, who had seen her daily for three weeks in their midst. All who had been admitted to her presence left her with tears of joy and devotion; her simple and modest behaviour, blended with her splendid enthusiasm, won every heart. Her manner and modesty, and the gay brightness of her answers, had also won the suffrage of the priests and lawyers, and the military were as much delighted as surprised at her good sense when the talk fell on subjects relating to their trade.

It was on or about the 20th of April 1429 that Joan of Arc left Poitiers and proceeded to Tours. The King had now appointed a military establishment to accompany her; and her two younger brothers, John and Peter, had joined her. The faithful John de Metz and Bertrand de Poulangy were also at her side. The King had selected as her esquire John d'Aulon; besides this she was followed by two noble pages, Louis de Contes and Raimond. There were also some men-at-arms and a couple of heralds. A priest accompanied the little band, Brother John Pasquerel, who was also Joan's almoner. The King had furthermore made Joan a gift of a complete suit of armour, and the royal purse had armed her retainers.

During her stay at Poitiers Joan prepared her standard, on which were emblazoned the lilies of France, in gold on a white ground. On one side of the standard was a painting representing the Almighty seated in the heavens, in one hand bearing a globe, flanked by two kneeling angels, each holding a fleur-de-lis. Besides this standard, which Joan greatly prized, she had had a smaller banner made, with the Annunciation painted on it. This standard was triangular in form; and, in addition to those mentioned, she had a banneret on which was represented the Crucifixion. These three flags or pennons were all symbolic of the Maid's mission: the large one was to be used on the field of battle and for general command; the smaller, to rally, in case of need, her followers around her; and probably she herself bore one of the smaller pennons. The names 'Jesu' and 'Maria' were inscribed in large golden letters on all the flags.

The national royal standard of France till this period had been a dark blue, and it is not unlikely that the awe and veneration which these white flags of the Maid, with their sacred pictures on them, was the reason of the later French kings adopting the white ground as their characteristic colour on military banners.

Joan never made use of her sword, and bore one of the smaller banners into the fight. She declared she would never use her sword, although she attached a deep importance to it.

'My banner,' she declared, 'I love forty times as much as my sword!'

And yet the sword which she obtained from the altar at Fierbois was in her eyes a sacred weapon.

CHAPTER II.
THE DELIVERY OF ORLEANS.

It will be now necessary to go back in our story to the commencement of the siege by the English of the town of Orleans, in order to understand the work which Joan of Arc had promised to accomplish. Orleans was the place of the utmost importance; not merely as being the second city in France, but as forming the 'tete du pont' for the passage of the river Loire. The French knew that were it to fall into the hands of the English the whole of France would soon become subject to the enemy.

The town was strongly fortified; huge towers of immense thickness, and three stories in height, surrounded by deep and wide moats, encircled the city. The only bridge then in existence was also strongly defended with towers, called 'Les Tournelles,' while at the end of the town side of the bridge were large 'bastilles,' powerful fortresses which dated from the year 1417, when Henry V. threatened Orleans after his triumphal march through Normandy. In 1421 the Orleanists defied the victor of Agincourt: again they were in the agony of a desperate defence against their invaders, ready to sustain all the horrors of a siege.

Equally keen and determined were the English leaders to take Orleans, which they rightly considered as the key of what remained unconquered to them in France. Both countries looked anxiously on as the siege progressed. Salisbury commanded the English; he had been up to this point successful in taking all the places of importance in the neighbourhood of Orleans, and that portion of the valley of the Loire was commanded by his forces, both above and below Orleans.

On the approach of the enemy, the inhabitants of Orleans turned out to strengthen the outer fortifications, and to place cannon and catapults on the walls and ramparts. The priests on this occasion worked as hard as the other citizens, and even the women and children helped with a will.

Besides Dunois, who commanded the besieged garrison, was Raoul de Gaucourt, who had defended Harfleur in 1415; he had but recently returned from imprisonment in England, and was burning to avenge his captivity. La Hire, Xaintrailles, Coulant, Coaraze, and Armagnac were among the defenders of Orleans. Many Gascons belonging to the Marshal-Saint Severe and soldiers from Brittany helped to swell the forces of the besieged.

It was on the 12th day of October (1428) that Salisbury crossed the Loire and established his besieging force at the village of Portereau, in front of the strongly defended bridge. In the meanwhile the besieged had razed the houses and the convent of St. Augustin, in order to prevent the enemy from entrenching themselves so near the city gates. Salisbury, however, threw up fortifications on the site of St. Augustin's, and placed a battery of guns opposite to the bridge and its 'bastilles,' whence he was able to bombard the town with huge stones. The English also placed mines below the bridge and the fortresses of the Tournelles.

On the 21st, an assault was made on the bridge and its defences, which was vigorously repulsed; the whole population were in arms, and manned the walls; the women fought by the side of their husbands and brothers. After a severe fight of four hours, the besiegers were forced to withdraw.

The Tournelles were now mined and counter-mined, and were soon found to be untenable. The besieged then abandoned this fortification, and retired further back towards the centre of the bridge, which, as well as its approaches, was defended by towers. Part of the bridge on the side near the English was blown up, and a drawbridge, which could be raised or lowered at pleasure, was thrown across the open space.

Salisbury was satisfied with the result of that day's fighting, for he knew that, once he had the command of the northern side of the tower, he could take it when necessary from that quarter. What he aimed at for the present was to prevent all communication between the town and the south of France. Holding the bridge, he could prevent relief from coming to the city, and when the moment arrived he would be able to throw his men with certain success upon it from the northern side.

The evening of the day in which he had made so successful an attack, Salisbury mounted into the Tournelles in order to inspect thence the city which lay beneath him. While gazing on it, a stray cannon shot struck him on the face; he was carried, mortally wounded, from the place. That fatal shot was said to have been fired by a lad, who, finding a loaded cannon on the ramparts, had discharged it. For the English, it was the deadliest shot of the whole war.

Readers of Shakespeare will remember that, in the first part of **Henry VI.**, the Master Gunner (no doubt that very 'Maitre Jean' whose fame was great in the besieged town) and his boy are introduced on the scene, and that the boy fires the shot which proved fatal both to Salisbury and Sir Thomas Gargrave. The prominent place given to this French Master Gunner in the English play shows what a high reputation Maitre Jean must have had, even among the English, at the siege.

Salisbury's death, occurring a few days after he received the wound, caused the siege to languish. Glansdale succeeded Salisbury in the command; but it was not until the doughty Talbot and Lord Scales appeared on the scene that siege operations recommenced with vigour.

The great pounding match then began again; the huge stone shot of the English, which weighed one hundred and sixty-four livres, came tumbling about the heads of the besieged, to which cannonade the French promptly replied by a heavy fire. They had a kind of bomb, of which they were not a little proud, wherefrom they fired iron shot of one hundred and twenty livres in weight. The Master of Gunners of Shakespeare's play, whose name was John de Monsteschere, made also extraordinary practice with his culverin; and he could pick off marked men in the Tournelles, as, for the misfortune of the English, had been proved in the case of Salisbury. At times Master John would sham dead, and, just as the English were congratulating themselves on his demise, would reappear, and again use his culverin with deadly effect.

On the last day but one of the year (1428), the English had been reinforced, and were now commanded by William de la Pole, Earl, and afterwards Duke of Suffolk, under whose command acted Suffolk's brother, John de la Pole, Lord Scales, and Lancelot de Lisle. In order to maintain touch with his troops posted at the Tournelles, Suffolk threw up flanking batteries on the northern side of the town. To Suffolk's already large force Sir John Fastolfe brought a force of twelve hundred men, in the month of January (1429).

The number of troops mustered by the besieged and besiegers was as follows:--

On the side of the English, there were quartered at the Tournelles five hundred men, under the command of Glansdale; three hundred under Talbot; twelve hundred with Fastolfe. Including those who had come with Suffolk at the commencement of the siege, the English force amounted to four thousand five hundred men.

On the side of the besieged, excluding the armed citizens, who were from three to four thousand strong, was a garrison numbering between six and seven hundred men; also some thousand soldiers had been thrown into the city between the middle of October 1428 and the January following.

Both in strength of position, and as regards the number of their troops, the French had the advantage. The comparative weakness of the English force--which, all told, could only count about four thousand men to carry on the siege--is to be accounted for by the garrisons which were left in the conquered places over the north and south of the country.

The siege was weakly conducted during the winter--a series of skirmishes from the bastilles or towers thrown up by the besiegers led to little result on either side; and it was not till the month of February that a decisive engagement took place.

Near Rouvray a battle was fought, which is known by the singular appellation of the Battle of the Herrings, from the circumstance that, at that Lenten season, a huge convoy of fish was being taken from the coast to Paris. In the fight, the fish-laden barrels were overthrown, and their contents scattered over the field; whence the name of the Battle of the Herrings. During this engagement, in which the French were defeated, fell, on the side of the French, two noble Scots--John Stuart, the Constable of Scotland, and his brother William.

After this action, the position of the besieged in Orleans became more perilous, and the citizens, despairing of help coming to them from Charles, were inclined to call in aid from the Duke of Burgundy. The east, north, and west of the city were covered by the bastilles or huge towers which the besiegers had thrown up, and from which they could bombard the place; and the pressure on the devoted city waxed ever stronger. By the month of April, Orleans was girdled by a chain of fortresses, from which the cannonade was incessant. The English gave names of French towns to these huge towers which threatened Orleans on every side; one they named Paris, another Rouen, and one other they called London.

The thirty thousand men, women, and children within the city walls were now beginning to suffer from the horrors of a long siege. In the town disturbances broke out, and the cry of treachery was heard--that sure precursor of the fears of the strong that the hardships of the siege would undermine the patriotism of their weaker citizens. But when things seemed at their worst, succour was near at hand.

During those winter months the Queen-mother, who had warmly interested herself in Joan of Arc's mission, had, in the Castle of Blois, been collecting troops and securing the services of some notable officers, including the Duke of Alencon. Towards the end of April Joan arrived at Blois from Poitiers, accompanied by the Archbishop of Rheims, Regnault de Chartres. On the 27th of April she left Blois on her first warlike expedition.

No certain account of the numbers of troops which accompanied the Maid has been kept. Monstrelet gives the numbers at seven thousand; but Joan, during her trial, asserted that she had between ten and twelve thousand men committed to her charge by the King. Joan's historian, M. Wallon, points out that this may be an incorrect entry made in the interest of the English at the trial, as they naturally would wish the relieving force to appear as large as possible. It has even been placed as low as three thousand. Among the officers who accompanied the Maid was a Gascon knight, named La Hire, half freebooter, half condottiere, a brave and reckless soldier, of whom it is recorded that, before making a raid, he would offer up the following prayer:--

'I pray my God to do for La Hire what La Hire would do for Him, if He were Captain and La Hire was God.'

From having been a mighty swearer, owing to Joan of Arc's influence La Hire broke off this habit, but, in order to give him some scope for venting his temper, Joan allowed him to swear by his stick.

These are but trivial details: still, they are of interest as showing what influence a simple village maiden like Joan was able to exert on those who, from their position and habits of life, might have been thought to be the last to tolerate such interference. So changed, it is said, had this rough warrior, La Hire, and many of his fellow-soldiers become in their habits while with the Maid, that they were happy to be able to kneel by the side of the sainted maiden and partake in her Lord's Sacrament of the Eucharist; and then to confess themselves to her good father confessor, Peton de Xaintrailles, the Marshal de Boussac, and the Seigneur de Rais.

Joan had the following letter despatched to the Duke of Bedford:--

'In the name of Jesus and Mary--You, King of England; and you, Duke of Bedford [Bethfort], who call yourself Regent of France; you, William de la Pole; you, Earl of Suffolk; you, John Lord Talbot [Thalebot]; and you, Thomas Lord Scales, who call yourselves Lieutenants of the said Bedford, in the name of the King of Heaven, render the keys of all the good towns which you have taken and violated in France, to the Maid sent hither by the King of Heaven. She is ready to make peace if you will consent to return and to pay for what you have taken. And all of you, soldiers, and archers, and men-at-arms, now before Orleans, return to your country, in God's name. If this is not done, King of England, I, as a leader in war, whenever I shall meet with your people in France, will oblige them to go whether they be willing or not; and if they go not, they will perish; but if they will depart I will pardon them. I have come from the King of Heaven to drive you out [bouter] of France. And do not imagine that you will ever permanently hold France, for the true heir, King Charles, shall possess it, for it is God's wish that it should belong to him. And this has been revealed to him by the Maid, who will enter Paris. If you will not obey, we shall make such a stir [ferons un si gros hahaye] as hath not happened these thousand years in France. The Maid and her soldiers will have the victory. Therefore the Maid is willing that you, Duke of Bedford, should not destroy yourself.'

And Joan finishes this strange effusion by proposing to Bedford that they should combine in making a holy war for Christianity!

This letter, written 'in the name of the Maid,' was dated on a Tuesday in Holy Week. The address ran thus: 'To the Duke of Bedford, so called Regent of the Kingdom of France, or to his Lieutenants, now before the town of Orleans.'

Doubtless the reference to the deed of arms which, once again at peace together, might be accomplished by the combined English and French armies, was an idea which seems to have floated in Joan's enthusiastic imagination, that the day might come when the two foremost nations in Christendom would fight together for the recovery of the Holy Sepulchre.

As might be expected, this letter was received by the English with gibes and jeers, which was pardonable; but what was not so was the bad treatment of the messenger who had brought it to the English camp. He was kept prisoner, and, if some rather doubtful French writers of the day are to be believed, it was seriously debated whether or not he should be burnt. Let us trust this is but an invention of the enemy.

Joan, before leaving Blois, insisted on the dismissal of all camp followers--such bad baggage was certainly well left behind, and could not have followed an army led by one who, night and morning, had an altar erected, around which her hallowed flags were placed, and where the Maid, and those willing, took the Sacrament at the head of the army. It must have been a striking sight during that spring-time--that army, led by a maiden all clad in white armour, and mounted on a black charger, surrounded by a brilliant band of knights, riding along the pleasant fields of Touraine, then in their first livery of brilliant green. And a striking sight it must have been, when, at the close of the long day's march, the tents were pitched and the altar raised, the officiating priests grouped about it and the sacred pictured standards waving above, while the solemn chant was raised, and the soldiers knelt around.

One can well think how ready were those soldiers to follow Joan wherever she would lead them, and it is not improbable that such a crusade as she dreamt of, had it been possible, in which the two nations, so closely connected by religious feeling, and so closely united by position, but so long enemies owing to the rapacity and greed of their kings, might have again placed the cross on the battlements of the Holy City, under the leadership of her whom her countrymen rightly called 'The Angelic.'

Joan rode out of Blois bearing her pennon in her hand, and as she rode she chanted the 'Veni Creator.' The sacred strain was taken up by those who followed, and thus passed the Maid forth on her first great deed of deliverance.

During the whole of the first night Joan remained, as was her custom when she had no women about her, in her armour.

It was the Maid's wish to enter Orleans from the northern side, but the officers with her thought this would be a great imprudence, and followed the opposite bank of the river. Passing through Beaugency and Meung, they went on by Saint Die, Saint Laurent, and Clery, without meeting with any attack from the enemy who occupied these places. On arriving at a place called Olivet, they were within the neighbourhood of the beleaguered city. Below them rose the English bastille towers; beyond, the walls, towers, and steeples of Orleans.

Joan had hoped that the city could have been entered without further difficulty; she now found that not only the river lay between her and the town, but that the English were in force on all sides. She wished that the nearest of these bastilles, at Saint Jean le Blanc, should be stormed, and the river forded there; but this scheme was judged by her companions-in-arms to be too perilous, and Joan had again to comply with the opinion of the officers.

Riding to the eastwards, and skirting the river some four miles below the town, she and her knights forded it at a spot where some low long islands, or 'eyots' as we call them on the Thames, lay in this part of the Loire. On one of these, called l'Isle aux Bourdons, the provisions and stores for the beleaguered city were shipped and transhipped, and carried down to Orleans when the wind lay in that quarter.

It was at Reuilly that Dunois met the Maid, still chafing from her thwarted plan of attacking the English in their stronghold at Saint Jean le Blanc, and she appears to have shown him her displeasure. While this interview took place the wind changed, and the provision boats, which, owing to the wind being contrary, had not been able to make the islands, were now enabled to leave the city. They soon arrived, were laden with provisions, corn, and even cattle embarked on them, and, when thus provisioned, returned to Orleans by the canal on the left bank of the Loire, and successfully arrived at the city end of the broken bridge, whence the provisions and live stock were passed into the town.

The river was too much in flood to allow of the army being taken across, nor could a bridge of boats be made, owing to the height of the waters. Joan, however, was determined to enter Orleans, flood or no flood, for she knew what the moral effect of her appearing to the townspeople would be. Accompanied by Dunois, La Hire, and some two hundred lances, just after darkness had hidden her movements from the enemy, she left Reuilly and entered the city.

Preceded by a great banner, the Maid of Orleans, as she may now be called, with Dunois by her side, and followed by her knights and men-at-arms, rode slowly through the streets, filled with a crowd almost delirious in its joy at welcoming within its walls its long-looked-for Deliverer. The people clung to her, kissing her knees and feet, and, according to the old chroniclers, behaved as if God Himself had appeared among them. So eager was the throng to approach her, that in the press one of her standards was set on fire by a flambeau. After returning thanks for the delivery of her countrymen in the cathedral, Joan was made welcome at the house of the treasurer of the imprisoned Duke of Orleans. This citizen's name was James Boucher; and here she lodged, with her brothers, and the two faithful knights who had accompanied her during her journey from Vaucouleurs to Chinon.

A vaulted room in this house is still shown, which purports to have been that occupied by the Maid of Orleans. If it is the same building it has been much modernised, although a beautiful specimen of the domestic Gothic of the early part of the fifteenth century, known as the house of Agnes Sorel, remains much in the condition that it must have been in during the famous year of deliverance, 1429.

Although Orleans, by the action of Joan of Arc, had been succoured for the time, the enemy was still at its gates, and Joan's mission was but half accomplished. The aspect of affairs since the 29th of April was, however, greatly changed in favour of the French, and the *roles* of besieged and besiegers changed. Joan's arrival had infused a fresh spirit of enthusiasm and patriotism into the citizens, and the English were no longer feared. We have Dunois's authority for the fact that whereas, up to that time, two hundred English could put eight hundred French to the rout, now five hundred French soldiers were prepared to meet the entire English army.

On the 13th of April, hostilities had recommenced. Four hundred men, commanded by Florent d'Illiers, made a sortie against the English near the trenches at Saint Pouair, driving them into their quarters. But the success was not followed up, and appears to have been undertaken without Joan of Arc's advice. To the heralds that she sent into the English camp only jeers and taunts were returned; and already the threat of burning her when caught was made use of. Joan was, however, not to be deterred by menaces and insults from doing all she could to prevent unnecessary loss of life. On one occasion she rode out half-way across the bridge, to where there stood a crucifix called La Belle Croix, within speaking distance of the English in the Tournelles. Thence she summoned Glansdale and his men to surrender, promising that their lives should be spared. They answered with derisive shouts and villainous abuse. Still commanding her patience, which was only equalled by her courage, and before returning to the town, she told them that, in spite of their boasting, the time was near at hand when they would be driven forth, and that their leader would never see England again. That they feared the Maid was evident, in spite of the insults with which they greeted her; at any rate, no attempt was made to attack her: even when almost alone, she came close to their fortifications.

Meanwhile Dunois left for Blois to bring up the bulk of the army, while Joan remained in Orleans, encouraging its inhabitants by her confidence, faith, and courage. The people, writes the chronicler of the siege, were never sated with the sight of the Maid: 'ils ne pouvaient saouler de la voir,' he graphically says.

A second ineffectual effort was made by Joan, this time at a place called the Croix Morin, to negotiate with the English, she again promising them quarter if they would capitulate, but, as might be expected, with no better result than before.

On the 2nd of May, followed by a vast throng, Joan of Arc rode out along the enemy's forts, and after closely inspecting their defences returned to vespers at the Church of Sainte-Croix. Certainly among the people there was no want of belief in, and enthusiastic devotion to, the Maid; but she had already enemies among the *entourage* of the King. We have already alluded to Tremoille's feelings with regard to her and her mission. A still more formidable enemy was the Chancellor of France, the Archbishop of Rheims, Regnault de Chartres; he and Tremoille worked in concert to undermine all the prestige which Joan's success in revictualling Orleans had caused at Court. The historian Quicherat, whose work on Joan of Arc is by far the most complete and reliable, considers this man to have been an astute politician, without any moral strength or courage. When with Joan of Arc, he seems to have shown firmness and even enthusiasm in her mission, but he sank into the *role* of a poltroon when her influence was withdrawn. Instead of hastening the despatch of the reinforcements from Blois to Orleans, he threw delay in the way; he seems to have hesitated in letting these troops join those under the Maid, for fear that were she to gain a thorough success his influence at Court would be weakened. When Joan fell into the hands of her foes, the Archbishop had the incredible baseness publicly to show his pleasure, declaring that her capture by the enemy was a proof of Divine justice.

It was not till the 4th of May, and not until Dunois had ridden in hot haste from Blois, that at length the aid, so long and eagerly expected, arrived.

Joan rode to meet the succouring army some two miles out of the city, bearing her flag, accompanied by La Hire and others of her knights. After a joyful meeting, they turned, riding right through the enemy's lines and along the fortified bastilles occupied by the English. Whether it was fear, or superstition mixed with fear, not a man from the English side stirred, although the English outnumbered the French. It seemed that a terror had seized on the enemy as they saw her, whom they called the Sorceress, ride by in her white panoply, bearing aloft her mystic banner.

The English had now run short of supplies, and eagerly awaited the arrival of Sir John Fastolfe, who was on his road to Orleans. Joan of Arc felt uneasy, lest she might not be able to cut off Fastolfe and his supplies, and she playfully threatened Dunois with his instant execution if he failed to tell her of the moment he learnt of his approach. Her anxiety was well founded, for the attack commenced before she had been apprised of it. She had lain down for a short repose one afternoon, when she heard the sounds of a cannonade. She instantly ordered her squire d'Aulon to arm her, as she must immediately attack the English; but whether those at the Tournelles, or the advancing force under Fastolfe, she could not yet tell.

While arming, a great clamour rang through the town: the enemy were said to be at hand, and the battle already engaged. Hastily throwing on her armour, with the assistance of her hostess and d'Aulon, she dashed off on her horse, and had only time to snatch her flag, as it was handed to her from a window, so impetuous was she to enter the fray.

As she galloped down the street the sparks flew from the stones, through the High Street and past the cathedral, and out by the Burgundy Gate. The action had already been raging, and the wounded were being borne back into the town. It was the first time the Maid came face to face with such grisly sights--the agony of the wounded, the blood and gaping wounds. Her squire, d'Aulon, who has left some record of that day, says how much she grieved over the wounded as they were carried past her; her beloved countrymen bleeding and dying affected her deeply. As her page writes, she said she could not see French blood without her hair rising with horror at the sight.

Before she reached the field the day had been lost and won, the English were in full retreat, and the battle now lay around the bastilles of Saint Loup. About a mile to the north-east of the town were the Englishmen; strongly entrenched, the place commanded that portion of the river which Talbot had garrisoned with some three hundred of his best troops. Joan now gave instructions that no aid should reach this portion of the English defences from the adjacent bastilles. All around the fight raged, and Joan was soon in the hottest of the engagement, encouraging her soldiers, her flag in her hand. Dismounting, she stood on the edge of the earthwork, beyond which the English were at bay.

Talbot, seeing his men hard pressed, gave orders for a sortie to be made from one of the other towers, named Paris, and thus cause a diversion, while another force attacked the French in their rear. This expedient, however, failed, for a fresh force appeared at this juncture from Orleans, led by Boussac and De Graville, who beat back the attack of the English. The English troops within the fortress of Saint Loup were slain or taken. Joan herself rescued some of these, and placed them under her protection; caring for them in the house she was staying in.

At the close of the day, on returning into the town, Joan told the people that they might count on being free from the enemy in five days' time, and that by that time not a single Englishman would remain before Orleans. No wonder that the joy-bells rang out in victorious clamour during all that night in May, the eve of the Ascension.

On the following day no hostilities occurred. Joan again had a letter sent to the English, summoning them as before to surrender and to quit their forts; she said this was the third and the last time that she could give them a chance of escaping with their lives. On this occasion she made use of a new way of communicating with the foe; she tied the letter to an arrow, which was discharged into the English lines. No answer was received in return.

It was now determined that the next attack against the English should be made from the left bank of the river, where they were strongly fortified at the Bastille des Augustins, a little further down the Loire than the Tournelles. On the opposite side this fortress communicated with the Boulevard of Saint Prive, as well as with the strong fortress of Saint Laurent, near which a small island, which exists no longer, called the Isle of Charlemagne, kept open their connections on both sides of the Loire. To the east, on the same side of the river, a fortress, that of Saint Jean le Blanc, which had been abandoned on the approach of Joan, had since been reoccupied by the English. It was at this spot that the next and all-important attack was directed to be made.

The French forces crossed the river over an island called Saint Aignan. The distance was so narrow between the river bank on the town side and this island, that a couple of boats moored together served as a bridge. When Saint Jean le Blanc was reached, it was found deserted by the English, Glansdale having left it in order to concentrate his forces at the Tournelles. Joan led the attack. At first the French fought badly; they had been seized by a panic, believing that a strong force of the enemy were coming down on them from Saint Prive. Rallying her men, Joan threw herself on the English, and drove them back into the Augustins. She was now eagerly followed by the soldiers.

The first barricade was carried in a hand-to-hand fight, and soon the French flags waved above the fortress so long held by the enemy. The few English able to escape retired to the Tournelles. Eager to carry on the success of the attack, and to prevent delay, Joan ordered that the fort of the Augustins be fired, with the booty it contained.

The victors, who only numbered three thousand strong, captured six hundred prisoners, one third were slain of the English, and two hundred French prisoners recovered.

This was the second occasion on which the Maid had carried all before her.

The day was closing, and the attack on the Tournelles had to be deferred for that evening. That night Joan of Arc said to her almoner: 'Rise early to-morrow, for we shall have a hard day's work before us. Keep close to me, for I shall have much to do, more than I have ever had to do yet. I shall be wounded; my blood will flow!'

This prophetic speech of the Maid is among the most curious facts relating to her life; for not only did she, during her trial at Rouen, tell her judges that she had been aware that she would be wounded on that day, and even knew the position beforehand of the wound, but that she had known it would occur a long time before, and had told the King about it. A letter is extant in the Public Library at Brussels, written on the 22nd of April (1429), by the Sire de Rotslaer, dated from Lyons, in which Joan's prophecy regarding her wound is mentioned. This letter was written fifteen days before the date (7th of May) of the engagement when that event occurred. A facsimile of the passage in this letter referring to Joan's prophecy appears in the illustrated edition of M. Wallon's *Life of Joan of Arc*.

Very early on the following day, Saturday, the 7th of May, it appears that an attempt was made to prevent the Maid from starting for the field, as, at a council held on the evening before by the officers, it had been considered more prudent, before renewing the attack on the English fortifications, to await fresh reinforcements from the King. When this was reported to Joan, she said: 'You have taken your counsel, and I have received mine,' and at break of day she was ready, armed and prepared for the attack. Before starting, her host wished her to eat some fish, an 'alose,' which had just been brought to him. 'Keep it,' said Joan with a smile, 'till the evening, and I will bring with me a "Godon" who will, eat his share of it.' This sobriquet of 'Godon' was evidently the generic term for the English, as far back as the early years of the fifteenth century, and may have been centuries before the French designation for our countrymen.

Thus, full of spirits and with a brave heart, the Maid rode off to meet the foe. When she reached the gate called Burgundy, she found it closed by order of De Gaucourt, Grand Master of the King's Household, who had done so at the instigation of those officers who wished the attack on the English deferred until fresh reinforcements arrived. But the Maid was not to be beaten and kept back even by barred gates.

'You are doing a bad deed,' she indignantly said to those about the gate, 'and whether you wish it or not, my soldiers shall pass.'

The gate was opened, and Joan, followed by her men, galloped to where some troops who had been left in possession of the fortifications taken on the previous day were stationed. The attack on the Tournelles commenced as soon as Joan arrived--it was then between six and seven in the morning. Meanwhile Dunois, La Hire, and the principal forces from the town came up. A desperate struggle ensued; both sides knew that, whatever the result, that day would decide the fate of Orleans--even that of the war.

The French were fighting under the eyes of their countrymen, who manned the walls, and under the guidance of a leader they already regarded as more than human--and never had they fought so well, during that long and bloody century of warfare, as they did on that day.

The English, on the other hand, knew that if they were beaten out of the Tournelles their defeat would be complete, and they too fought with desperate courage.

Down into the ditches rushed the French, and up the sides of the glacis; scaling-ladders were placed against the walls, to which the men upon them clung like a swarm of bees. The defenders met them with showers of arrows and shot, and hurled them back with lance and hatchets. Constantly beaten back, they returned as constantly to the charge. For six hours this fight lasted, and weariness and discouragement fell on the French. Joan, who had been all these hours in the thick of the engagement, seeing her men were losing heart, redoubled her efforts; and, helping to raise a scaling-ladder, she placed it against the parapet of one of the towers. While thus engaged she was struck by a bolt from a cross-bow, between her shoulder and neck. The wound was a severe one; she fell, and was carried out of the press. Although she suffered acutely, she had the nerve to draw the arrow from the wound. She refused to have the wound 'charmed,' as some of those standing around her suggested, saying she would sooner die than do anything that might be displeasing in the sight of Heaven. A compress, steeped in oil, was then applied, and it staunched the bleeding. She was faint and unnerved, and, as she seemed to feel her death was near, made her confession to her priest.

Still the Tournelles held out in spite of these repeated attacks, and Dunois, as the shadows lengthened, was on the point of calling back his forces and sounding the retreat. Joan, in the meanwhile, had been withdrawn from the fighting, and placed in a meadow at some distance from the carnage; but when she heard that the troops were about to be recalled from their attack on the Tournelles, she seemed to forget her wound, and, making her way to Dunois, implored him not to give up the fight. She assured him that she was certain they would even yet be victorious. In a few stirring sentences she rallied the men to fresh efforts, and told them that now or never would they conquer; the English, she declared, could not hold out much longer. Mounting her horse, and with flag unfurled, she again led the van; to those near her she said, 'Watch my standard; when it reaches the walls the place will be ours.'

The struggle that ensued was fierce and decisive. Inspired by the valour of Joan, the French, who appeared as fresh as before her wound, stormed the bastions and towers of the Tournelles with tremendous energy. Reinforcements had meanwhile arrived from the town, and these attacked the Tournelles in the rear. Passing over the broken arches of the bridge by means of ladders thrown across the masonry, the first man to reach the other bank was a knight of Rhodes, Nicolas de Giresme. Attacked from two sides, the English still held the Tournelles with bull-dog tenacity; but the sight of the witch and sorceress, as they considered Joan, and who they thought had met with a mortal hurt, leading the soldiers with unabated courage, caused a panic to spread through their ranks; and when a sudden shout of victory proclaimed that the white and golden banner had at length struck the walls of the fortress, the doom of the Tournelles had arrived.

Clear above the din of battle rang out the triumphant voice of the Maid: 'The victory is ours!' she cried.

Seeing the day was lost, the English now attempted to escape destruction by swimming the river; others threw themselves on a bridge, which, however, having been set on fire by the French, only caused those who hoped to cross to fall either into the flames or into the river below.

Glansdale, the English leader, who had grossly insulted Joan but a few days before, was among those who were drowning in the Loire. Seeing his peril, Joan of Arc attempted to save him, but Glansdale was swept, before her aid could reach him, down the stream, never more to return to his own land again, as Joan had prophesied.

Five hundred English perished either in the Tournelles or were drowned in attempting to escape; the rest were made prisoners by the French.

Darkness had now fallen, and although Joan had been taking part in the battle for more than a dozen hours, and had besides been grievously hurt, she would not leave the field till late in the night, in case the English at the Bastille of Saint Laurent should be inclined to avenge the fall of the Tournelles, and the victory over their comrades. But for that day, at all events, the English had had enough of fighting: 'ils n'en avaient une vouloir' for more, as the old chronicler quaintly expresses himself.

Riding back across the bridge which the citizens had in the meanwhile partially restored, Joan re-entered the city which her splendid courage had rescued from the English. 'God knows,' writes Perceval de Cagny, 'with what joy she was received'; and our English historian of those days, Hall, has left the following graphic account of the joy that went out from the people of Orleans to their saviour:--

'After the siege was thus broken up, to tell you what triumphs were made in the city of Orleans, what wood was spent in fire, what wine was drunk in houses, what songs were sung in the streets, what melody was made in taverns, what rounds were danced in large and broad places, what lights were set up in the churches, what anthems were sung in chapels, and what joy was showed in every place--it were a long work, and yet no necessary cause. For they did as we in like case would have done; and we, being in like estate, would have done as they did.'

All that day Joan of Arc had eaten nothing, and her strength must have been more than mortal to have sustained the heat, fatigue, and, above all, the anguish of her wound. At length she was able to find some repose with her kind hosts, and, after taking a little bread dipped in wine, she retired to enjoy her well-earned rest.

Orleans was now delivered, as the citizens found on waking the next morning after the battle, when the joyful news spread through the town that the English had abandoned the bastilles on the northern side of the city, leaving all their sick, stores, artillery, and ammunition. That day Lord Talbot must have used expressions probably not as poetical as those put into his mouth in the play of *Henry VI.*; but doubtless far more forcible--for it was now that he, for the first time, felt the bitterness of defeat, the shame of turning his back on his enemy; that enemy whom, until now, he had, after so many victories, almost grown to despise.

'My thoughts are whirled like a potter's wheel;   I know not where I am, nor what I do: A witch, by fear, not force, like Hannibal,   Drives back our troops, and conquers as she lists.'

But although retire he had to, Talbot's retreat was made in perfect order, and in a kind of defiant fashion. Ranging his forces near to and facing the town, he seemed inclined to make a further stand, if not to carry out an attack against the city. Joan was prepared to repel such an attack, but the English contented themselves with a mere feint, a military demonstration.

The day was a Sunday, and Joan, ever loath to fight on that day, refused to give the signal for attack, saying that if the enemy chose to begin an engagement they would be met and defeated; but that she could not sanction fighting on that holy day. Prepared for whatever might occur, the Maid of Orleans then ordered that Mass should be said at the head of her troops.

When the religious act was over:

'Look,' she said, 'whether the English have their faces or their backs turned to us.'

And when she heard that they were in full retreat on Mehun-sur-Loire, she added, 'Let them depart, in God's name: it is not His wish that you should attack them to-day, and you will meet them again.'

After an hour's halt, the English continued to retreat, previously setting fire to their bastilles, and carrying their prisoners with them.

The day that saw the deliverance of Orleans was held for centuries as a national day of rejoicing in the town, and seldom have the citizens of any place had better cause for celebrating so joyful and honourable an event. The siege which Joan had thus brought to an end began on the 12th of October (1428), and ended on the 8th of May (1429). Ten days had sufficed for the heroic Maid to raise the English blockade.

Throughout France the effect of the news of the deliverance of Orleans was prodigious; and although most of the English, no doubt, believed that the result was owing to the instrumentality of the powers of darkness, many saw in it the finger of God.

When the great news reached Paris on the 10th of May, Fauconbridge, a clerk of Parliament, made the following note in his register:--'Quis eventus fuerit novit Deus bellorum'; and on the margin of the register he has traced a little profile sketch of a woman in armour, holding in her right hand a pennon on which are inscribed the letters I.H.S. In the other hand she holds a sword. This parchment may still be seen in the National Archives in Paris.

Joan, having accomplished her undertaking, lost no time in returning to the King at Chinon.

CHAPTER III.
THE CORONATION AT RHEIMS.

Leaving the now free and happy town to jubilate in its deliverance from the enemy, Joan of Arc went by Blois and Tours to Chinon. At Tours the King had come to meet the Maid. When within sight of the King, Joan dismounted and knelt before him. Charles came forward bareheaded to meet her, and embraced her on the cheek; and, to use the words of the chronicler, made her 'grande chere'. It was on this occasion that the King bestowed on Joan of Arc the badge of the Royal Lily of France to place in her coat-of-arms. The cognizance consisted of a sword supporting a royal crown, with the fleur-de-lis on either side.

Joan now strongly urged the King to lose no time, but at once go to Rheims, to be crowned. The fact of his being crowned and proclaimed King of France would add infinitely to his prestige and authority; he would then no longer be a mere Dauphin or King of Bourges, as the English and Burgundians styled him. But now Joan found how many at Court were lukewarm. The council summoned to deliberate on her proposal alleged that the King's powers and purse would not enable him to make so long and hazardous an expedition. Joan used every argument in favour of setting out forthwith for Rheims: she declared that the time given to her for carrying out her mission was short, and, according to the Duke of Alencon's testimony, she said that after the King was crowned she would deliver the Duke of Orleans from his captivity in England, but that she had only one year in which to accomplish this task; and therefore she prayed that there might be no delay in starting for Rheims.

Charles was now staying at the Castle of Loches, that gloomy prison-fortress whose dungeons were to become so terribly notorious in the succeeding reign. Joan, whose impatience for action carried her beyond the etiquette of the Court, entered on one occasion into the King's private apartment, where the feeble and irresolute monarch was consulting with his confessor the Bishop of Castres, Christophe d'Harcourt, and Robert de Macon. Kneeling, the Maid said:--

'Noble Dauphin, hold not such long and so many councils, but start at once for Rheims, and there receive your crown.'

'Do your voices inspire this advice?' asked the King's confessor.

'Yes,' was the answer, 'and with vehemence.'

'Then,' said the Bishop, 'will you not tell us in the King's presence in what way your voices communicate with you?'

To this Jesuitical query, Joan, in her simple and straightforward manner, answered the priest, that when she met with people who doubted the truth of her mission she would retire to her room and pray, and then voices returned and spoke to her:--'Go forward, daughter of God, and we will assist you,' and how hearing those voices and those words she would rejoice and take courage, and only long that her then state of happiness might last always. While telling them these things she seemed a being transformed, surrounded by a something Divine and holy.

It was not unnatural that the King and his councillors should hesitate before making up their minds to undertake the journey to Rheims, for the English were posted in force at Beaugency, at Meun, where Talbot was encamped, and at Jargeau. They also held a strong position on the Loire; it would be difficult to reach Rheims without encountering some of their forces. Jargeau had been attacked, indeed, by Dunois and Xaintrailles, but unsuccessfully; and there was real danger in going northwards while the English were still so plentiful and so strongly entrenched in the towns of the centre and south of France. Another reason for delaying the journey to Rheims and the ceremony of the coronation, was that some time must elapse before the princes and great nobles, who would have to take part in the coronation, could assemble at Rheims.

Joan, thus thwarted in her wish of marching directly on to Rheims, suggested driving the English from their fortresses and encampments on the Loire. To this scheme the royal consent was obtained, and the Duke of Alencon was placed in command of a small force of soldiers. Joan directed the expedition, and it was ordered that nothing should be done without the sanction of the Maid.

In a letter, dated the 8th June, 1429, written by the young Count of Laval, who met Joan of Arc in Selles in Berri, the place of rendezvous for the expedition, is a pleasant notice of the impression the heroine caused him. He describes her as being completely armed, except that her head was bare. She entertained the Count and his brother at Selles. 'She ordered some wine,' he writes, 'and told me that I should soon drink wine with her in Paris.' He adds that it was marvellous to see and hear her. He also describes her leaving Selles that same evening for Romorantin, with a portion of her troops. 'We saw her,' he writes, 'clothed all in white armour excepting her head; her charger, a great black one, plunged and reared at the door of her lodging, so that she could not mount him. Then she said, "Lead him to the Cross," which cross stood in front of the church on the high road. And then he stood quite still before the cross, and she mounted him; then as she was riding away she turned her face to the people who were standing near the door of the church; in her clear woman's voice she said:--"You priests and clergy, make processions, and pray to God for our success." Then she gave the word to advance, and with her banner borne by a handsome page, and with her little battle-axe in her hand, she rode away.'

The church before which this scene took place at Selles-sur-Cher still exists, a fine massive building, dating from between the eleventh and thirteenth centuries; but the old cross that stood before it, to which Joan of Arc's black charger was led, has long ago disappeared.

In my opinion, this graphic description of the Maid of Orleans, written by Guy de Laval to his parents, is the best that has come down to our day of the heroine. There is to us a freshness about it which proves how deeply the writer must have been stirred by that wonderful character; it shows too that, with all her intensely religious and mystic temperament, Joan of Arc had a good part of sprightliness and **bonhomie** in her character, which endeared her to those whose good fortune it was to meet her.

The incident of the black charger standing so still beside the cross, and the figure of the Maid, mystic, wonderful, in her white panoply, with her head bare--that head which, in spite of no authentic portrait having come down to us, we cannot but imagine a grand and noble one--make up a living picture of historic truth, far above the fancies evolved out of the brains of any writer of fiction--for is it not romance realised?

The eagerness to accompany Joan of Arc in this expedition of the Loire was great. The Duke of Alencon wrote to his mother to sell his lands in order that money might be raised for the army. The King was unable or unwilling to pay out of his coffers the expenses of the campaign. From all sides came officers and men eager for new victories under the banner of the Maid.

Joan led the vanguard, followed by Alencon, de Rais, Dunois, and Gaucourt. At Orleans they were joined by fresh forces under Vendome and Boussac. On the 11th of June the army amounted to eight thousand men. Jargeau was the first place to be attacked. Here Suffolk, with between six and seven thousand men, all picked soldiers, had established himself. Inferior in numbers, the English had the advantage over the French in their artillery. In the meanwhile, Bedford, who had news of Suffolk's peril, sent Fastolfe to Jargeau, with a fresh force of five thousand men. But for some reason or other Fastolfe seemed in no hurry to come to Suffolk's assistance; he lost four days at Etampes, and four more at Jauville. Some alarm seems to have been felt among the French troops at the news of Fastolfe's approach. Joan mildly rebuked those who showed anxiety by saying to them: 'Were I not sure of success, I would prefer to keep sheep than to endure these perils.'

The faubourgs of the town of Jargeau were attacked and taken, but before storming the place, Joan, according to her habit, sent a summons to the army. She bade the enemy surrender: doing so, he would be spared, and allowed to depart with his side-arms; if he refused, the assault should be made at once. The English demanded an armistice of fifteen days: hardly a reasonable request when it is remembered that Fastolfe, with his reinforcements, might any day arrive before Jargeau. Joan said they might leave, taking their horses with them, but within the hour. To this the English would not consent, and it was decided to attack upon the following morning.

The next day was a Tuesday; the signal was given at nine in the morning. Joan had the trumpets sounded, and led on the attacking column in person. Alencon appears to have thought the hour somewhat early; but Joan overruled him by telling him that it was the Divine will that the engagement should then take place. 'Travaillez,' she repeated, 'Travaillez! et Dieu travaillera!'

These words may well be called Joan of Arc's life motto, and the secret of her success. 'Had she,' she asked Alencon, 'ever given him reason to doubt her word?' And she reminded him how she had promised his wife to bring him, Alencon, back safe and sound from this expedition. Joan seems throughout that day's fighting to have watched over the Duke's safety with much anxious care; at one hour of the day she bade him leave a position from which he was watching the attack, as she told him that if he remained longer in that place he would get slain from some catapult or engine, to which she pointed on the walls. Hardly had the Duke left the spot when a Seigneur de Lude was struck and killed by a shot from the very engine about which Joan had warned Alencon.

Hour after hour raged the attack; both Joan and Alencon directed the storming parties under a heavy fire. A stone from a catapult struck Joan on her helmet as she was in the act of mounting a ladder--she fell back, stunned, into the ditch, but soon revived, and rising, with her undaunted courage, she turned to hearten her followers, declaring that the victory would be theirs. In a few more moments the place was in possession of the French. Suffolk fled to the bridge which spanned the Loire: there he was captured. A soldier named William Regnault beat him to the ground, but Suffolk refused to yield to one so low in rank, and is said to have dubbed his victor knight before giving him up his sword. Besides Suffolk, a brother of his was taken, and four or five hundred men were killed or captured. The place was pillaged. The most important of the prisoners were shipped to Orleans.

The following day Joan returned to Orleans with Alencon, where they remained two days to rest their men, after which they proceeded to Meun. This was a strongly fortified town on the Loire, about an equal distance from Orleans on the west and from Jargeau on the east.

The first success of the French was the occupation of a bridge held by the English. They then descended the river, and attacked the town of Beaugency. This town had been abandoned by the English garrison, who had thrown themselves into the castle. Here it was that the army of the Loire was joined by the Constable de Richemont, who could be almost considered as a little monarch in his own territory of Brittany. This magnate appears to have been a somewhat unwelcome addition to Joan and Alencon's army. He was, however, tolerated, if not welcomed. Alencon and the Constable, who had till now been at enmity, were reconciled by Joan's influence, and she paved the way for a reconciliation between Richemont and the King.

It was high time that all the French princes should be reconciled, for the danger from the invaders was still great even in the immediate circle of the Court and army. A strong body of men was known to be on the way from Paris, under the command of Fastolfe, and Talbot was marching to meet him with a force from the Loire district; they soon met, and together proceeded directly upon Orleans. Fastolfe appears to have been disinclined to attack, his force being smaller than that of the French; but Talbot was beside himself with rage at having to retreat from Orleans, and swore by God and St. George that, even had he to fight the enemy alone, fight he would. Fastolfe had to give way to the fiery lord, although he told his commander that they had but a handful of men compared to the French; and that if they were beaten, all that King Henry V. had won in France with so much loss of life would be again lost to the English.

Leaving some troops to watch the English garrisons in the castle of Beaugency, Joan marched against the English. The hostile armies met some two miles between Beaugency and Meun. The English had taken up a place of vantage on the brow of a hill; their archers as usual were placed in the front line, and before them bristled a stockade. The French force numbered about six thousand, led by Joan of Arc, the Duke of Alencon, Dunois, Lafayette, La Hire, Xaintrailles, and other officers.

It was late in the day when heralds from the English lines arrived with a defiant message for the French. Joan's answer was firm and dignified. 'Go,' she said to the heralds, 'and tell your chiefs that it is too late for us to meet to-night, but tomorrow, please God and our Lady, we shall come to close quarters.'

The English were still strongly fortified in the little town of Meun. A portion of their army left Beaugency in order to effect a junction with their other comrades, and in perfect order Talbot commenced his retreat on Paris, taking the northern road through the wooded land of La Beauce. They were closely followed by the French, but neither army had any idea how near they were to one another till a stag, startled by the approach of the French, crossed the English advanced guard. The shouts of the English soldiers on seeing the stag gallop by was the first sign the French had of the propinquity of their foes. A hasty council of war was held by the French commanders. Some were for delay and postponing the attack until all their forces should be united; and these, the more prudent, pointed out the inferiority of their force to that of the enemy, arguing that a battle under the circumstances, in the open country, would be hazardous. Joan of Arc, however, would not listen to these monitions. 'Even,' she cried, 'if they reach up to the clouds we must fight them!' And she prophesied a complete victory.

Although, as ever, anxious to command the attack, she allowed La Hire to lead the van. His orders were to prevent the enemy advancing, and to keep him on the defensive till the entire French force could reach the ground. La Hire's attack proved so impetuous that the English rearguard broke and fled back in confusion. Talbot, who had not had time, so sudden and unexpected had been the French attack, to place his archers and defend the ground, as was his wont, with palisades and stockades, turned on the enemy like a lion at bay. Fastolfe now came up to Talbot's succour; but his men were met by the rout of the rearguard of the broken battle, and the fugitives caused a panic among the new-comers. In vain did Sir John attempt to rally his men and face the enemy. After a hopeless struggle, he too was borne off by the tide of fugitives. One of these, an officer named Waverin, states the English loss that day to have amounted to two thousand slain and two hundred taken, but Dunois gives a higher figure, and places the English killed at four thousand.

This battle of Patay was the most complete defeat that the English had met with during the whole length of that war of a hundred years between France and England; and, to add to its completeness, the hitherto undefeated Talbot was himself amongst the taken.

'You little thought,' said Alencon to him, when brought before him, 'that this would have happened to you!'

''Tis the fortune of war,' was the old hero's laconic answer.

The effects of this victory of Patay on the fortunes of the English in France were greater than the deliverance of Orleans, and far more disastrous, for the French had now for the first time beaten in the open field their former victors. The once invincible were now the vanquished, and the great names of Crecy, Poitiers, and Agincourt had lost their glamour. When the news was known that the English under Talbot and Fastolfe had been beaten, and that the great commander for so many years the terror of France had been made a prisoner, and that these mighty deeds had been accomplished by the advanced guard of the French army under the inspiration of the Maid of Orleans, the whole country felt that the knell of doom of the English occupation in France had rung.

There is an anecdote relating to Joan of Arc at Patay that should find a place here. After the battle, and while the prisoners were being marched off by the French, Joan was distressed to see the brutality with which those captives unable to pay a ransom were treated. One poor fellow she saw mortally wounded by his captors. Flinging herself from her saddle, she knelt by the side of the dying man, and, having sent for a priest to shrive him, she remained by the poor fellow's side and attended to him to the end, and by her tender ministrations helped him to pass more gently over the dark valley of death.

Michelet discovered this story in the deposition of Joan of Arc's page, Louis de Contes, who was probably an eye-witness of the scene.

With this brilliant victory at Patay closed Joan of Arc's short but glorious campaign on the Loire. Briefly, this was the career of her victories:--On the 11th of June the Maid attacked Jargeau, which surrendered the next day. On the 13th she re-entered Orleans, where she rallied her troops. On the 15th she occupied the bridge at Meun, and the following day she attacked Beaugency, which yielded on the day after. The English had in vain hoped to relieve Jargeau: they arrived too late. After the fall of Beaugency they fell back, and were defeated at Patay on the 18th.

A wonderful week's work was this campaign, ordered and led by a maiden of eighteen. What made Joan of Arc's success more remarkable is the fact that among the officers who served under her many were lukewarm and repeatedly foiled her wishes. And it is not difficult to trace the feeling of jealousy that existed among her officers; for here was one not knight or noble, not prince, or even soldier, but a village maiden, who had succeeded in a few days in turning the whole tide of a war, which had lasted with disastrous effects for several generations, into a succession of national victories. This professional jealousy, as one may call it, among the French military leaders was fomented and aggravated by the perfidious counsellors about the King. The only class who thoroughly appreciated and were really worthy of the Maid and her mission, were the people. And it is still by the people that everlasting gratitude and love of the heroic Maid are most deeply felt.

While Joan was gaining a succession of victories on the Loire, the indolent King was on a visit to La Tremoille at his castle of Sully-sur-Loire. Accompanied by Alencon and the Constable Richemont, Joan repaired to Sully. She had promised to make the peace between Charles and Richemont, and as the Constable had brought with him from his lands in Brittany fifteen hundred men as a peace-offering, the reconciliation was not a matter of much difficulty. La Tremoille saw with an evil feeling the ever-growing popularity of Joan, and feared her daily increasing influence with the King; but he could not prevent the march on Rheims, much as he probably wished to do so. It was arranged that the army should be concentrated at Gien. From Gien, Joan addressed a letter to the citizens of Tournay, a town of doubtful loyalty to Charles, and much under the influence of the Burgundian party. She summoned in this letter those who were loyal to Charles to attend the King's forthcoming coronation.

On the 28th of June the King and Court left Gien, on their northern march. That march was not a simple matter, for a country had to be traversed in which the towns and castles still bristled with English garrisons, or with doubtful allies. Auxerre belonged to the Burgundian party, always in alliance with the English; Troyes was garrisoned with a mixed force of English and Burgundians; and the strongly fortified places on the Loire, such as Marchenois, Cosne, and La Charite, were still held by the English troops. Charles' army had no artillery; it was therefore out of the question to storm or besiege towns however hostile, and the counsellors and creatures of the King urged him not to risk the dangers of a journey to Rheims under such disadvantageous circumstances.

Joan, wearied out by the endless procrastination and hesitation of the King, left him, and preferred a free camp in the open fields to the purlieus of the Court, with its feeble sovereign and plotting courtiers. Joan of Arc on this occasion may be said to have 'sulked,' but she showed her usual common sense in what she did, and her leaving the Court seems to have given the vacillating King a momentary feeling of shame and remorse. Orders were issued that the Court should be moved on the 29th of June.

The royal army which started on that day for Rheims numbered twelve thousand men; but this force was greatly increased on its march. By the side of the King rode the Maid of Orleans; on the other side of the King, Alencon. The Counts of Clermont, of Vendome, and of Boulogne--all princes of the blood--came next. Dunois, the Marechal de Boussac (Saint-Severe), and Louis Admiral de Culan followed. And then, in a crowd of knights and captains, rode the Seigneurs de Rais, de Laval, de Loheac, de Chauvigny, La Hire, Xaintrailles, La Tremoille, and many others.

Before the town of Auxerre a halt was called: it was still under the influence of the English and Burgundians. A deputation waited upon Charles, provisions were sent to the army, but the town was not entered. Outside its fortifications the army rested three days, after which it continued its march to Saint-Florentin, whose gates swung open to the King; thence on to Brinon l'Archeveque, whence Charles forwarded a messenger with a letter to his lieges at Rheims, announcing his approach.

On the 4th of July the royal force had reached Saint-Fal, near Troyes. Joan of Arc despatched a messenger summoning that place to open its gates to the King; but Troyes was strongly garrisoned by a force of half English half Burgundian soldiers, and these had sent for succour to the English Regent, the Duke of Bedford. The army of the King arrived before the gates of the town on the 4th of July; a sally was made by the hostile garrison, but this was driven back. **Pour-parlers** ensued. The King's heralds were informed by the garrison officers that they had sworn to the Duke of Burgundy not to allow, without his leave, any other troops to enter their gates. They went further, and insulted the Maid of Orleans in gross terms, calling her a 'cocquarde'--whatever that ugly term may mean.

The situation was embarrassing. How could the town be taken without a siege train and artillery? But to leave it in the rear, with its strong garrison, would be madness. The King's men were in favour of retiring and abandoning the expedition to Rheims. There happened to be within the town of Troyes at this time a famous monk of the preaching kind, named Father Richard. Father Richard had been a pilgrim, and had visited the Holy Land, and had made himself notorious by interminable sermons, for he was wont to preach half-a-dozen hours at a time. Crowds had listened to him in Paris and other places. The English, who probably thought his sermons insufferably long, or too much leavened with French sympathies, drove him out of Paris, and he had taken refuge at Troyes. The monk had heard much of Joan of Arc, and was eager to see and speak with her, but his enthusiasm was mixed with a religious and even superstitious fear in regard to the heroine. He was allowed to enter the royal precincts, and approached the Maid of Orleans with many a sign of the cross, and with sprinkling of holy water. Seeing the good man's terror, Joan told him to approach her without fear.

'Come forward boldly!' she said to the monk. 'I shall not fly away!'

And after convincing him that she was not a demon in any way, she made him the bearer of a letter from her to the people in the town. The negotiations between the army and the burghers lasted five days; the town refusing to admit the King, and the King unwilling to pass the town, but unable to take it by force. Charles was on the point of giving up the attempt to reach Rheims when one of his Council pointed out that as the expedition had been undertaken at the instigation of Joan of Arc, it was only fair her judgment should now be followed, and not that of any one else. Joan was summoned before the Council, when she solemnly assured the King that in three days' time the place would be taken.

'If we were sure of it,' said the Chancellor, 'we would wait here six days.'

'Six days!' said the Maid. 'You will enter Troyes to-morrow.'

Mounting her horse, the Maid rode into the camp, and ordered all to prepare to carry out a general assault on the next morning. Anything that could be used in the shape of furniture and fagots, to make a bridge across the town ditches, was collected. Joan, who had now her tent moved up close to the moat, worked harder, says an eye-witness, than any two of the most skilful captains in preparing the attack. She directed that fascines should be thrown into the moat, across which the troops were to pass to the town.

Early next day everything was in readiness for the attack, but at this juncture, just as she was preparing to lead the storming party, the Bishop of Troyes, John Laiguise, attended by a deputation of the principal citizens, came from the town with offers of capitulation. The people were ready to place themselves at the King's mercy, owing probably to the terror the preparations made by Joan of Arc on the previous evening had inspired them with, mixed, too, with the superstitious dread they felt for her presence. Had not even the English soldiers declared that, when attacked by the terrible Maiden, they had seen what appeared to be flights of white butterflies sparkling all around her form! How could these good people of Troyes hope to withstand such a power? To add to this fear, it was remembered by the citizens of Troyes that in it had been signed and concluded the shameful treaty by which Charles VII. had been disinherited from his crown and possessions. The people therefore gave in without further struggle. The conditions of capitulation were soon arranged. The burghers were granted the immunity of their persons and their goods, and certain liberties for their commerce. All those traders who held any office at the hands of the English government were to continue the enjoyment of these offices or benefices, with the condition of taking them up again at the hands of the King of France. No garrison would be quartered upon the town, and the English and Burgundian soldiers were to be allowed to depart with their goods.

The next day--the 10th of July--Charles and his host entered Troyes in state, the Maid of Orleans riding by the side of the King, her banner displayed as was her custom.

When, as had been arranged in the treaty of capitulation, the foreign soldiers began to leave the place with bag and baggage (goods), Joan was indignant at finding that some of these so-called goods were nothing less than French prisoners. This was a thing that she could not tolerate, treaty or no treaty; and, placing herself at the gate of the town, she insisted that her imprisoned countrymen should be left in her charge. The King naturally felt obliged to gratify her; so he released the captives, and paid their ransom down. Before leaving Troyes the next day, William Bellier, who had been Joan's host at Chinon, was left as bailiff of the place, along with other officers.

Thence the army moved on by way of Chalons. Though still in the hands of the English, a deputation of clergy and citizens met the King, and placed themselves at his orders.

While in the neighbourhood of Chalons, Joan of Arc met some friends who had arrived from Domremy; among them were two old village companions, Gerardin d'Epinal and John Morel, to whom she gave her red dress. In conversation with these she said that the only dread she had in the future was treachery: a dread which seems to point in some strange prophetic manner to the fate which was so soon to meet her at Compiegne.

It was on the evening of the 16th of July that the royal host at length came in sight of the massive towers of the great cathedral church of Rheims. It was at Sept Saulx, about eight miles' distance from Rheims, that the King waited for a deputation to reach him from the town. Rheims was still filled with the English and Burgundian adherents, and had Bedford chosen to throw, as he could well have done, a force into that place, Charles might yet have been prevented from entering its gates. Perhaps Bedford did not believe in the possibility of Charles arriving at his goal, and had counted on the King's well-known weakness and indecision, and on the hesitation of such men as La Tremoille and others of his Council. The Regent had received assurances from the officials in Rheims that they would not admit Charles. But after what passed at Troyes and at Chalons, Charles had not long to wait for a favourable answer from his lieges at Rheims. Indeed, the deputation which met him at Sept Saulx were effusive in their good offices and entreaties that the King should forthwith enter his good city of Rheims.

The Archbishop (Regnault de Chartres), who had preceded the King by a few hours to his town, came out to meet the King at the head of the corporation and civic companies. From all sides flocked crowds eager to welcome the King, and even more the Maid of Orleans. In those days the people's cry of joy and triumph was 'Noel!'--but why that cry of Christmas joy had become the popular hosanna, it is not easy to conjecture.

Throughout that night the preparations for the coronation were feverishly made both within and without the cathedral. On the 17th of July, with all the pomp and ceremony that the church and army could bestow, the King was crowned and anointed with the holy oil which four of his principal officers had brought to the cathedral from the ancient abbey church of Saint-Remy.

There exist few grander fanes in Christendom than the great cathedral of Rheims. The thirteenth century, so prolific of splendid churches, had expended all its wealth of lavish decoration on the gorgeous portal, with its array of saints and sovereigns, under which passed Charles VII. of France, with the Maid of Orleans on his right hand. Hurried as had been the preparations for the ceremonial, the even then ancient and venerable rites must have deeply impressed the spectators, and the semi-sacred act was carried out with scrupulous care--the King crowned and anointed with the holy oil, surrounded on his throne by the ecclesiastical peers and high dignitaries of the Church, and waited on by the secular peers during the crowning and after at the coronation banquet.

At length was accomplished the darling wish of Joan of Arc's heart, for now her King was regarded and sanctioned by all true French persons as King of France, by the grace of God and Holy Church.

When the King received the crown from the hands of the Archbishop, a peal of trumpets rang out, with such a mighty volume of sound that the very roof of the cathedral seemed to shake again. Ingres, in his striking picture of Joan of Arc, now in the gallery of the Louvre, represents her standing by the high altar, clad in her white panoply of shining steel, her banner held on high; below bows in prayer her confessor, the priest Pasquerel, in his brown robes of the Order of Augustin; and beyond stand her faithful squire and pages. The heroine's face is raised, and on it sits a radiant look of mingled gratitude and triumph. It is a noble idea of a sublime figure.

When the long-drawn-out ceremony came to an end, and after the people had shouted themselves hoarse in crying 'Noel!' and 'Long live King Charles!'--Joan, who had remained by the King throughout the day, knelt at his feet and, according to one chronicle, said these words:

'Now is finished the pleasure of God, who willed that you should come to Rheims and receive your crown, proving that you are truly the King, and no other, to whom belongs this land of France.'

Many besides the King are said to have shed tears at that moment.

That seemed indeed the moment of Joan of Arc's triumph. The ***Nunc Dimittis*** might well have then echoed from her lips; but in the midst of all the rejoicing and festivity at this time Joan had saddened thoughts and melancholy forebodings as to the future. While the people shouted 'Noel!' as she rode through the jubilant streets by the side of the King, she turned to the Archbishop, and said: 'When I die I should wish to be buried here among these good and devout people.'

And on the prelate asking her how it was that at such a moment her mind should set itself on the thought of death, and when she expected her death to happen, she answered: 'I know not--it will come when God pleases; but how I would that God would allow me to return to my home, to my sister and my brothers! For how glad would they be to see me back again. At any rate,' she added, 'I have done what my Saviour commanded me to do.'

Her mission was indeed accomplished: that is to say, if her mission consisted of the two great deeds which while at Chinon she had repeatedly assured her listeners she was born to accomplish. These were, first, to drive the English out of Orleans, and thereby deliver that town; the second, to take the King to Rheims, where he would receive his crown. The other enterprises, such as the wish to deliver the Duke of Orleans from his captivity in England, and then to wage a holy war against the Moslems, may be left out of the actual task which, encouraged by her voices,

Joan had set herself to accomplish. But the two great deeds had now been carried out--and with what marvellous rapidity! In spite of all the obstacles placed in her path, not only by the enemies of her country, but by those nearest to the ear of the King, Orleans had been delivered in four days' time, the English host had been in a week driven out of their strongholds on the Loire, and defeated in a pitched battle! The King unwillingly, and with many of his Court opposed to the enterprise, after passing through a country strongly occupied by the enemy without having lost a man, had by the tact and courage of Joan of Arc been enabled to reach Rheims; and after this successful march he had received his crown among his peers and lieges, as though the country were again at peace, and no English left on the soil of France. What was still more surprising was, that all these things should have been accomplished at the instigation and by the direction of a Maid who only a few months before had been an unknown peasant in a small village of Lorraine. How had she been able not only to learn the tactics of a campaign, the rudiments of the art of war, but even the art itself? No one had shown in these wars a keener eye for selecting the weakest place to attack, or where artillery and culverin fire could be used with most effect, or had been quicker to avail himself of these weapons. No one saw with greater rapidity--(that rarest of military gifts)--when the decisive moment had arrived for a sudden attack, or had a better judgment for the right moment to head a charge and assault. How indeed must the knights and commanders, bred to the use of arms since their boyhood, have wondered how this daughter of the peasants had obtained the knowledge which had placed her at their head, and enabled her to gain successes and reap victories against the enemy, which until she came none of them had any hope of obtaining. They indeed could not account for it, except that in Joan of Arc was united not only the soul of patriotism and a faith to move mountains, but the qualities of a great captain as well. That, it seems to us, must have been the conclusion that her comrades in arms arrived at regarding the Maid of Orleans.

Dunois stated that until the advent of the Maid the French had no longer the courage to attack the English in the open field, but that since she had inspired them with her courage they were ready to attack any force of the army, however superior it might be. This testimony was confirmed by Alencon also: he declared that in things outside the province of warfare she was in every respect as simple as a young girl; but in all that concerned the science of war she was thoroughly skilled, from the management of a lance in rest to that of marshalling an army; and that as regarded the use of artillery she was eminently qualified. All the military commanders, he said, were amazed to see in her as much skill as could be expected in a seasoned captain who had profited by a training of from twenty to thirty years. 'But,' added the Duke, 'it is principally in her use of artillery that she displays her most complete talent.' And he proceeds to bear his high tribute to her goodness of heart, which she displayed on every possible occasion.

Although her physical courage enabled her to face the greatest perils and personal risks, she had a horror of bloodshed, and though her spirit was 'full of haughty courage, not fearing death nor shrinking distress, but resolute in most extremes,' she never entered battle but bearing her banner in her hand; and to the last day of her appearance on the field she strove with all her great moral force to induce the rude and brutal men around her to become more humane even in the hurly-burly of the din of battle. All unnecessary cruelty and bloodshed made her suffer intensely, and we have seen how she ministered to the English wounded who had fallen in fight. As far as she could she prevented pillage, and she would only promise her countrymen success on the condition that they should not prey upon the citizens of the places they conquered. Even when she had passed the day fasting on horseback, Joan would refuse any food unless it had been honourably obtained. As a child she had been taught to be charitable and to give to the needy, and she carried out these Christian principles when at the head of armies; the 'quality of mercy' with her was ever present. She distributed to the poor all she had with her, and would say, with what truth God knows, 'I have been sent for the consolation of the poor and the relief of the needy.' She would take upon herself the charge of the wounded; indeed, she may be considered as the precursor of all the noble hearts who in modern warfare follow armies in order to alleviate and help the sick and wounded. And she tended with equal care and sympathy the wounded among the enemy, as well as those of her own side.

This is no invention, no fancy of romance, but the plain truth; for there can be no disputing the testimony of those who followed Joan of Arc and saw her acts.

Regarding herself, Joan of Arc said she was but a servant and an instrument under Divine command. When people would avow that such works as she had carried out had never been done in former times, she would simply say: 'My Saviour has a book in which no one has ever read, however learned a scholar he may be.'

In all things she was pure and saint-like, and her wonderful life, as Michelet has truly said of it, was a living legend. Had she not been inspired by her voices and her visions to take up arms for the salvation of her country, Joan of Arc would probably have lived and ended her obscure life in some place of holy retreat. An all-absorbing love for all things sacred was her ruling idiosyncrasy. From her childhood her delight was to hear the church bells, the music of anthems, the sacred notes of the organ. Never did she miss attending the Church festivals. When within hail of a church it was her wont, however hurried the march, to enter, attended by any of the soldiers whom she could induce to follow her, and kneel with them before the altar. At the close of some stirring day passed in the midst of the din of battle, and after being for hours in the saddle, she would, ere she sought rest, always return thanks to her God and His saints for their succour.

Joan also loved to mix in the crowd of poor citizens, and begged that the little children should be brought to her. Pasquerel, her confessor, was always told to remind Joan of Arc of the feast days on which children were allowed to receive the Communion, in order that she too might receive it with these innocents.

The army has probably ever been the home of high swearing: the expression in French of 'ton de garnison' is an amiable way of referring to that habit of speech; and we all know ancient warriors whose conversation is thickly larded with oaths and profanity. This habit Joan of Arc seems to have held in great abhorrence. We have seen how she got La Hire to swear only by his stick; to another officer of high rank, who had been making use of some strong oaths, she said: 'How can you thus blaspheme your Saviour and your God by so using His name?' Let us hope her lesson bore fruit.

Throughout the land Joan of Arc was now regarded as the Saviour of France. Nor at this time did the King prove ungrateful. In those days nobility was highly regarded. It brought with it great prestige, and much benefit accrued to the holders of titles. Charles now raised the Maid of Orleans to the equal in rank of a Count, and bestowed upon her an establishment and household. The grateful burghers of Orleans, too, loaded her with gifts, all which honours Joan received with quiet modesty. For herself she never asked anything. After the coronation at Rheims, when the King begged her to make him a request, the only thing she asked was, that the taxes might be taken off her native village.

Her father, who came to see her at Rheims, had the satisfaction of carrying back this news to Domremy.

Although both King and nobles vied in paying honours to Joan of Arc, it was from the common people, from the heart of the nation, that she received what seems to have amounted to a feeling approaching adoration. Wherever she passed she was followed by crowds eager to kiss her feet and her hands, and who even threw themselves before her horse's feet. Medals were struck and worn as charms, with her effigy or coat-of-arms struck on them. Her name was introduced into the prayers of the Church.

Joan, although touched by these marks of affection, never allowed the people, as far as in her power lay, to ascribe unearthly influence to her person. When in the course of her trial the accusation that the people had made her an object of adoration was brought as a proof of her heresy, she said: 'In truth I should not have been able to have prevented that from being so, had God not protected me Himself from such a danger.'

CHAPTER IV.
THE CAPTURE.

We must now glance at the movements of the English since the deliverance of Orleans and their defeat at Patay, and the French King's coronation.

What proves the utter demoralisation of the English at this time is that the Regent Bedford was not only afraid of remaining in Paris, but had also taken refuge in the fortress of Vincennes. He was so poor that he could not pay the members of Parliament sitting in Paris. Like other bodies receiving no pay, the Parliament declined to work. So restricted were all things then in Paris that when the child-king (Henry VI.) was brought from London to be crowned there, not enough parchment could be found on which to register the details of his arrival.

For want of a victim to assuage his ire, the Regent disgraced Sir John Fastolfe, whom he unknighted and ungartered, in order to punish him for the defeat at Patay; and he wrote that the English reverses had been caused by 'a disciple and lyme of the Feende, called the Pucelle, that used fals enchantements and sorcerie.'

The Regent, whose degrading of Fastolfe and vituperation of Joan of Arc did not serve to help, applied to his powerful brother-in-law, the Duke of Burgundy, for aid. Burgundy came to the Regent's assistance, bringing a small force with him from Picardy. Then Bedford bethought him of his powerful relation in England, Henry Beaufort, the Bishop of Winchester. Most opportunely for the Regent, the Bishop had collected an army for the suppression of the Bohemian Hussites. The Regent implored his uncle, the Bishop, to send this army for the defence of the English and their interests, now in such dire jeopardy. Winchester was a mean, avaricious prince, and his aid had to be bought. A treaty was signed on the 1st of July, in which Winchester promised to bring his troops to his nephew's assistance; but he delayed stirring till the middle of that month. It pleased the crafty Bishop to know that his great wealth made him all-powerful in England; for the English Protector, the Duke of Gloucester, was a mere cipher compared to Winchester; and now that his other nephew, the Protector of France, was in distress, he could dictate his own terms to both. It was not until the 25th of July that Winchester at length arrived with his army in Paris. Then Bedford breathed more freely, and left the capital with an army of observation to watch the movements of the French King.

It was now the earnest wish of Joan of Arc that Charles should march direct on Paris, and perhaps had he done so he might have entered that city with as little difficulty as he had entered Rheims; for if once the King of France had appeared in person, many of the wealthy citizens, as well as the majority of the common people, would have welcomed him. Charles, however, as usual vacillated, and the precious moment slipped by.

Philip (called 'the Good'), Duke of Burgundy, was at this time one of the most powerful princes of Christendom. In addition to his titular domain, he held the wealthy provinces of Burgundy, including Brabant, Flanders, Franche-Comte, Holland, Namur, Lower Lorraine, Luxembourg, Artois, Hainault, Zealand, Friesland, Malines, and Salines. This much-territoried potentate was at the present juncture coquetting both with Bedford and with Charles, playing one against the other. To the former he promised an army, but only contributed a handful of men; to the latter he made advances of friendship, as false as the man who made them.

Joan had despatched two letters of a conciliatory tone to the Duke of Burgundy from Rheims. The original of one of these is to be seen in the archives at Lille. Like most of Joan of Arc's letters, it commences with the name of Jesus and Mary. As Joan could not write, the only portion of this letter which bears the mark of her hand is the sign of the Cross placed at the left of those names at the top of the document. She strongly urged the Duke in these letters to make peace with the King; she appeals on the score of his relationship with Charles, to his French blood, in order to prevent further bloodshed, and to aid the rightful King. While waiting some definite answer from the Duke, the King went to Vailly-sur-Aisne from Rheims. He arrived at Soissons on the 28th of July, and Chateau Thierry on the next day. Montmirail was reached on the 1st of August, Provins on the 2nd. It will be seen that, instead of marching straight upon Paris, the King was making a mere detour from Rheims towards the Loire.

It was soon evident that Charles and his civil councillors had no intention of advancing direct upon Paris, and were merely marching and counter-marching until they could, as they trusted, get the Duke of Burgundy to join them.

In the meanwhile, Bedford saw his opportunity, and made prompt use of it. Early in the month of August he issued a proclamation calling on all the subjects of Henry of England in France and Normandy to rally round their liege lord. Leaving Paris on the 25th of July, Bedford marched to Melun with a force of ten thousand men. Melun was reached on the 4th of August. On the day after Bedford's arrival at Melun a letter was sent by Joan of Arc to her friends at Rheims, announcing that the King's retreat on the Loire would not be continued by his Majesty. The King had, in fact, met with a check to his advanced guard at Bray-sur-Seine. Charles had, she informed her correspondents, concluded a truce of fifteen days with the Duke of Burgundy, at the expiration of which the Duke had promised to surrender Paris to the King. But, she adds, it could not be certain whether the Duke would keep to his promise. She concludes her letter by saying that should the treaty not hold good, then the army of the King would be able to take active measures.

This letter is vaguely dated from a lodging on the road to Paris. It was, she knew, necessary to be near the capital at the close of the period stipulated by Burgundy, and the royal army accordingly took the northern road, leading to Paris.

On the 7th of August the royal force reached Coulommiers; on the 10th La Ferte Milon, and on the 11th Crespy-en-Valois. Bedford, apprised of this change in the movements of his foe, sent off an insulting letter to Charles, whom he addressed as 'Charles who called himself Dauphin, and now calls himself King!' The Regent reproaches the King for having taken the crown of France, which he said belonged to the rightful King of France and of England, King Henry; and he then styles the Maid of Orleans 'an abandoned and ill-famed woman, draped in men's clothes and leading a corrupt life.' He bids Charles to make either his peace with him or to meet him face to face. Altogether a most rude, abusive, and ungallant letter for one prince to send to another. This letter reached Charles at Crespy-en-Valois on the 11th of August. Bedford was then close at hand, and eager to provoke the King into attacking him.

Charles contented himself with pushing on his advanced guard as far as Dammartin, remaining himself at Lagny-le-Sec.

During the 13th of August skirmishes took place between the advanced guards of the armies, but without any result.

Bedford now returned to Paris--in order to collect more troops, some said, others that he had found the French too strong to attack. The towns and villages around Paris, hearing of these events, and that the English had returned to the capital, showed now their readiness to join the French cause.

On his way to Compiegne news reached the French King that Bedford had left Paris and marched on Senlis. On the 15th of August the French attacked the English at dawn. Their army, formed into companies, was commanded by Alencon, Rene d'Anjou, the King, who had with him La Tremoille, and Clermont. Joan of Arc was at the head of a detachment with Dunois and La Hire. The English held a strong position, which they had made still more so by throwing up palisades and digging ditches.

What appeared destined to be a great engagement ended in a mere skirmish. Neither Charles nor Bedford were eager to pit all on a stake, and both preferred to play a waiting game. Charles retired on Crecy, while Joan of Arc remained in the field. She had done all that courage and audacity could to induce the English to attack. She had ridden up to their palisades and struck them with the staff of her banner. But nothing would make the English fight that day; and the next, Joan had the mortification of watching the retreat of the English upon Paris. Joan had nothing now left her to do but to rejoin the King at Crecy.

On the 17th the King received the keys of the town of Compiegne, and there he was welcomed on the next day with much loyalty. It was during his stay at Compiegne that Charles heard the welcome news that the people of Senlis had admitted the Count of Vendome within their walls, and had bestowed on him the governorship of their town. Beauvais had also shown its loyalty, had made an ovation in honour of the King, and had ordered the ***Te Deum*** to be sung, greatly to the annoyance of the Bishop of that place--Peter Cauchon--a creature of the Anglo-Burgundian faction, of whom we shall hear a good deal later on.

Charles remained at Compiegne until the expiration of the term during which the treaty with the Duke of Burgundy relating to the disposal of Paris remained open; but the negotiations ended in Burgundy contenting himself with sending to Charles, John of Luxembourg and the Bishop of Arras with words of peace. Arrangements were projected that in order to come to a general peace the Duke of Savoy was to be called in as mediator. In the meanwhile a truce was proposed, which was to last until Christmas, with the proviso that the town of Compiegne should be ceded to Burgundy during the continuance of the armistice. No allusion appears to have been made regarding the fate of Paris.

Joan of Arc, knowing that without Paris all that she had fought for and obtained would soon again be lost, resolved to see what she could do without coming to the King for assistance. She bade Alencon be ready to accompany her, as she wished, so she expressed it, to see Paris at closer quarters than she had yet been able to do.

Joan of Arc left Compiegne accompanied by the Duke of Alencon on the 23rd of August, taking a strong force with them. At Senlis they collected more troops; on the 26th they arrived at Saint Denis. Here they were joined by the King, who may be supposed to have felt some shame at not having started with them from Compiegne; he came very unwillingly, it is said, for all that.

Bedford left Paris precipitately for Normandy, owing to the discovery of a plot having been started to make over Rouen to the French. This event must have opened the Regent's eyes to the uncertain tenure the English held even in the old duchy of their kings. Bedford had left Louis of Luxembourg in Paris to command its garrison of two thousand English soldiers. De L'Isle Adam was in command of the Burgundian soldiers. In addition to Luxembourg, who was a bishop (of Therouanne) as well as a soldier, Bedford had given charge of the joint command to an English officer named Radley. The Bishop summoned the Parliament in order that it should swear fealty to King Henry VI. The town walls and ditches were carefully repaired and renewed. Guns were placed on the towers, walls, and batteries; immense quantities of ammunition of iron and stone were piled ready at hand, to be used for the defence of all the gates and approaches of the city. The moats were deepened, and by dint of threats and menace, and by frightening the people as to the terrible revenge the French King would take on the town and its people when it fell into his power, the citizens were cajoled into being made the agents of their natural enemies, and in sheer terror helped to strengthen the defences of their town.

During the first days of the siege only a few unimportant skirmishes took place between besieged and besiegers. Joan of Arc was indefatigable, and with her keen eye sought out the likeliest place where an assault might be successfully carried; but she lacked troops for storming such strong outworks as Paris then had. The capital was not only defended by walls and towers, but the English held both the upper and lower banks of the Seine.

From Saint Denis no assistance came from the King, and it was only on the 8th of September that, having received reinforcements, Joan of Arc was at length enabled to make a determined attack. It was a very high and holy day in the Church Calendar--the Feast of the Virgin's Nativity--and, not unmindful of the sacredness of that feast-day, Joan of Arc had determined to make a general attack; for 'the better the day the better the deed!' was her feeling on that anniversary. In those times the western limit of Paris was where now the wide thoroughfare of the Avenue de l'Opera runs from north to south. The walls of the city erected under Charles V., flanked by huge moats and protected by double fortress towers, each tower having a double drawbridge, made any attack almost a forlorn hope. The Regent's departure from Paris points to the little fear he felt that Paris could be taken by assault; and in this matter Bedford judged rightly.

Whether or not Joan felt that some Divine assistance would enable her to surmount the barriers that lay between her and the town she was so determined to win back for her King, we cannot say. She fought below the walls with a courage which, if the others had equalled, might have made Paris their own. The attacking force was divided into two parts--one, commanded by Joan, Rais, and De Gaucourt, was to attack the city at the Gate of Saint Honore; the other, led by Alencon and Clermont, was to cover the assailants, and prevent any sorties being made by the garrison.

Joan's impetuous onslaught successfully carried the first barriers and the boulevard in front of the gate; but here she met with a check--the heavy gates were barred, nor could she prevail on the enemy to make a sortie.

Joan of Arc, carrying her flag, dashed, under a heavy fire, into the ditch, followed by a few of the most courageous of the soldiers. The ditch was a deep but a dry one; and rising on the further side, close beneath the town walls, was a second and a wider moat, full of water. Here, unable to advance, but unwilling to retire, Joan of Arc and her followers were exposed to a murderous hail of shot, arrows, and other missiles. Sending for fagots and fascines to be cast into the moat, in order to enable a kind of bridge to be thrown across, while probing with the staff of her banner the depth of the water, Joan was struck by a cross-bow bolt, which made a deep wound in her thigh. Refusing to leave the spot, she urged on the soldiers to fill the ditch. The day was waxing late, and the men, who had been fighting since noon, were nearly exhausted. The news of Joan having been wounded caused a kind of panic among the French. There came a lull in the fighting, and the recall was sounded. Joan had almost to be forced back from before the walls by the Duke of Alencon and other of the officers. Placed upon her horse, she was led back to the camp, Joan protesting the whole time that if the attack had only been continued it would have been crowned with success. The spot where the heroine is supposed to have been wounded is near where now stands Fremiet's spirited statue of the Maid of Orleans, between the Rue Saint Honore--named in later days after the gate she had so gallantly attacked--and the Gardens of the Tuileries.

Within the town a great fear had fallen on the citizens, divided as they were between the hope of their countrymen forcing their way into the city and fear as to how they would be treated by Charles should he be victorious. Perhaps, had Joan of Arc's urgent entreaties of continuing the attack been more vigorously responded to by the other French commanders, she might have been in the end successful. At any rate Joan herself was of that opinion.

The following day she was, in spite of the previous evening's failure and her wound, as urgent as ever for further fighting; and again and again implored Alencon to renew the attack. It seems the Duke was on the point of complying, when there appeared on the scene Rene d'Anjou and Clermont, sent by the King with the order for the Maid's immediate return to Saint Denis. There was nothing to do but to obey, but it must have been a bitter disappointment to the brave maiden when she turned her back on Paris. Alencon did his best to encourage her in the hope that it might yet fall. He gave orders for a bridge to be thrown across the Seine at Saint Denis, in order to make a fresh attack on the city from that quarter. However, on the next night this bridge was ordered by Charles to be removed, and with its destruction fell any hopes Joan might still have entertained of being able to take Paris.

All the blame of the want of success of the army before Paris was now laid at the door of Joan of Arc; and the creatures of the Court, who had long waited for an opportunity of this kind to show their bitter jealousy of the heroine, now made no secret of their enmity. Foremost of these was the Archbishop of Rheims, who now, in spite of Joan of Arc's entreaties, was allowed by the King to make a truce with the enemy. Another powerful foe was La Tremoille, who (as has been pointed out by Captain Marin in his work on Joan of Arc) thought it to be against his personal influence that the French should take Paris. La Tremoille had shown, from Joan's first appearance at Court, his entire want of confidence in her mission. He had unwillingly, after the examination of the Maid by the doctors and lawyers at Poitiers, conformed to the King's wish that a command should be given her in the army. He had done all in his power to induce the King not to undertake the expedition to Rheims. He had told the King, when nothing else could be urged against the journey, that there was no money in the royal coffers, and that consequently the soldiers would not receive their pay. As it turned out, volunteers offered their services gratuitously to escort Charles to his crowning. At Auxerre, La Tremoille concluded a treaty with the citizens, which prevented Joan from taking that town. At Troyes he tried to create a like impediment; but here he was foiled, for Troyes capitulated. After the coronation, he persuaded Charles not to go to Paris, but to go instead to linger in his castle on the Loire; and thereby prevented what might then have proved a successful attack on the capital. And he again succeeded in thwarting the Maid of Orleans when he resisted her wish to make a second attack upon Paris. Later on it was La Tremoille who tried to make Joan of Arc fail at the siege of Saint Pierre-le-Moutier. When she was unsuccessful before La Charite-sur-Loire, and when the blame of that failure was laid at Joan's door, La Tremoille for very shame was obliged publicly to acknowledge the heroic zeal with which she had carried out the operations of that siege. The higher Joan's popularity rose among the people and in the army, the more her two bitter enemies, La Tremoille and the Archbishop of Rheims, shared between them their jealous dislike.

Thus, even before her capture and trial, Joan of Arc met with some of her worst foes among those whose duty it was to have been her staunchest friends and helpers; and, deplorable to say, among her own countrymen.

Charles left Saint Denis on the 13th of September. Before his departure, Joan of Arc performed an act which indicated that she felt her mission to be finished. In the old fane of Saint Denis, the tomb-house of the long line of French kings, she solemnly placed her armour and arms at the foot of an image of the Holy Mother, near the spot where were kept the relics of the Patron Saint of France. By that act of humility she seemed to wish to show her abnegation of any further earthly victory by the aid of arms.

We have now arrived at the turning-point of Joan of Arc's successes, and although the heroine is even more admirable in her days of misfortune and suffering than in those of her triumphs, when she led her followers on from victory to victory, the course of her brief life now darkens rapidly, and the approaching fate of the brave-hearted maiden is so terrible that it requires some courage to follow her to the very end, glorious as that end was, and bright with its sainted heroism.

The King's return journey from Compiegne to Gien was so hurried that it almost resembled a flight. Avoiding the towns still doubtful in their loyalty to him, Charles sped from Lagny to Bovins, then to Bray, Courtenay, Chateau-Regnaut, and Montargis, arriving at Gien on the 21st of September. Ere this time there could be little doubt of the Duke of Burgundy's unwillingness to abide by his pledge, and restore Paris to Charles. The Duke and Bedford had in fact already come to terms. The Regent resigned to Burgundy the Lieutenancy of the country, keeping only the now empty title of Regent and the charge of Normandy. The result of the King's withdrawal from the neighbourhood of Paris, and his hurried march, or rather retreat, to Gien, was that the English felt that there was now no longer any fear of their being drawn out of the capital. They promptly marched on and occupied Saint Denis, pillaging that town and carrying off as a trophy the arms which Joan of Arc had placed by the shrine of Saint Denis, in the ancient basilica of Dagobert.

The other towns, which had so recently returned to their allegiance to Charles, were again abandoned to the English, who punished them by levying large ransoms on the citizens. The surrounding country was laid waste, and Joan of Arc had the mortification of seeing that, without any attempt being made to defend her people, the places which had so shortly before been the scene of her triumphs were now allowed to be reoccupied by the English and their allies. Normandy, Picardy, and Burgundy were once more in possession of the enemy.

At length Joan obtained Charles' permission to attack La Charite, where the enemy were in force, and from whence they threatened the French forts on the Loire. At Bourges she assembled a few troops, and in company with the Sire d'Albret she laid siege to Saint Pierre-le-Moutier. Then, although feebly supported, Joan led the first column of attack. This attacking column might have been called a forlorn hope, so few men had she with her. The little party were repulsed, and at one moment her squire, d'Aulon, saw that his brave mistress was fighting alone, surrounded by the English. At great peril she was rescued from the melee. Asked how she could hope to succeed in taking the place with hardly any support, she answered, while she raised her helmet, 'There are fifty thousand of my host around me,' alluding to the vision of angels that in moments of extreme peril she relied on. D'Aulon in vain urged her to beat a retreat, and retire to a place of safety; she insisted on renewing the attack, and gave orders for crossing the moat on logs and fascines. A roughly constructed bridge over the fosse was then made, and after a desperate struggle the fortress was taken.

This occurred early in the month of November (1429). A few years ago a stained-glass window commemorative of the Maid of Orleans having saved the church in Saint Pierre-le-Moutier (it had been converted by the besieged into a warehouse for the goods and chattels of the citizens) was placed in the building she had preserved from destruction.

The next siege undertaken by Joan of Arc was that of La Charite--a far larger and more strongly garrisoned town than the other. La Charite was held by one Peter Grasset, who had been its governor for seven years. It was not only strongly defended by fortifications, but fully victualled for a prolonged siege. Joan and her little army had not the material necessary for carrying on such a siege as that of La Charite would require--the very sinews of war were wanting. Charles would not or could not contribute a single ecu d'or, and Joan had to solicit help and funds from the towns. In the public library at Riom is preserved the original letter addressed by the Maid of Orleans to 'My dear and good friends the clergy, burghers, and citizens of the town of Riom.' It was sent to that place on the 9th of November from Moulins. In this letter, the only one to which is affixed the Maid's signature, spelt 'Jehonne,' possibly signed by herself, she says that her friends at Riom are aware of how the town of Saint Pierre-le-Moutier had been taken, and she adds that she has the intention of driving out (de faire vider) the other towns hostile to King Charles. She begs the citizens of Riom, in order to accomplish this, to provide her with the means of pushing forward the siege of La Charite, and asks them to supply her with powder, saltpetre, sulphur, bows and arrows, cross-bows, and other material of war, having exhausted all her stock of such things in the late siege. Whether or not the burghers of Riom were able to carry out Joan's wishes is not known. The town of Bourges, however, provided funds out of its customs, and Orleans also sent soldiers and artillerymen ('joueurs de coulverines') to the Maid's army for the siege of La Charite.

But in spite of all efforts Joan of Arc was destined to fail in this undertaking. No doubt her enemies at Court helped to thwart all her attempts at raising a sufficient force to beleaguer so strong a place of arms, and seeing her hopes of taking La Charite by assault vanish, Joan of Arc relinquished the undertaking.

The remainder of that winter Joan of Arc passed in what must have tried her high spirit sorely--inaction.

Accompanying the Court, she went from Bourges to Sully-sur-Loire, and revisited Orleans. In the latter town we find some traces of her passage, and some further traits of her sweet nature, and of that simplicity which had endeared her so deeply to the hearts of the people: a disposition no success altered, no disappointment embittered. What was the chief charm of her character was this simplicity, her entire freedom from self-glorification, her horror of it being imagined that she was a supernatural or miraculous being, even when those supernatural and miraculous powers were considered as coming direct to her from Heaven--in fact, to use a slang but expressive phrase, her utter freedom from humbug. This is one of the most marked features of her character, although not the most glorious or salient to those who are dazzled by her triumphs and extraordinary career.

When she was told by people that they could well understand how little she feared being in action and under fire, knowing that she had a charmed life, she answered them that she had no more assurance of not being killed than the commonest of her soldiers; and when some foolish creatures brought her their rosaries and beads to touch, she told them to touch these themselves, and that their rosaries would benefit quite as much as if she had done so.

On one occasion at Lagny she was asked to resuscitate a dead child. One of the greatest of the French nobles wrote to ask her which of the rival Popes was the true one. When asked on the eve of a battle who would be victor, she answered that she could no more tell than any of the soldiers could. A woman named Catherine de la Rochelle, who assumed the power of knowing where money was hidden, was commanded by the King to take Joan of Arc into her confidence. The latter soon discovered that Catherine was a fraud, and refused to have anything to do with her. Catherine had suggested going to the Duke of Burgundy to arrange a peace between him and the French King, to which proposition Joan of Arc very sensibly said that it seemed to her that no peace could be made between them but at the lance's point. Joan had seen too much of the duplicity of the Duke to believe in any of his treaties and promises.

The early months of the year 1430 were months of anxiety for the citizens of Orleans and the other towns which had thrown off the English allegiance. The truce made between Burgundy and France expired at Christmas of the former year, but was renewed till Easter. Early in the year, the burghers of Rheims implored help of Joan of Arc, and not of the King, thus proving how far greater trust was placed in the hands of the Maid of Orleans, by such a town as Rheims, than in the goodwill of the King.

Twice during the month of March did Joan have letters written to reassure them of aid in case of need. 'Know,' she says in a letter dated the 16th of March, 'that if I can prevent it you will not be assailed; and if I cannot come to your rescue, close your gates, and I will make them [the English] buckle on their spurs in such a hurry that they will not be able to use them.'

In the second letter to the people of Rheims, written at Sully on the 28th of March, Joan tells them that they will soon hear some good news about herself. This good news referred no doubt to her return to the field, for we find that by the end of that month she was again on the march.

It was early in the month of April, 1430, that Joan of Arc left the Court and rode to the north, on what was to prove her last expedition. It is said that while at Melun, during Easter week, she was told by her voices that she would be taken prisoner before St. John's Day.

It was at Lagny that an incident occurred which formed one of the accusations brought against the Maid by her judges, and to which reference may now be made. A freebooter, named Franquet d'Arras, had, at the head of a band of about three hundred English freelances, held all the country-side in terror round about Lagny. Hearing of this, being in the neighbourhood of Lagny, Joan of Arc gave orders that Franquet and his band should be attacked. The French were in number about equal to the English. After a stubborn fight, the English were all killed or captured. Among the latter was the chief of the robbers, Franquet d'Arras. It was proved before the bailiff and justices of Lagny that Franquet had not only been a thief, but a murderer, and he was consequently condemned to die. Joan of Arc wished that he should be exchanged for a French prisoner, but this French prisoner had meanwhile died. The justices of Lagny insisted on having their sentence carried out, to which Joan at length unwillingly gave way, and Franquet met with his deserts. We cannot see how the Maid was to blame in this affair; but this thing was one of the accusations which helped to bring her to the stake.

On the 17th of April the truce agreed to between King Charles and Burgundy came to an end. At this time the town of greatest strategical importance to Burgundy was that of Compiegne. Holding Compiegne, the Duke of Burgundy held the key of France. King Charles, with his habitual carelessness, had been on the point of handing over Compiegne to the Duke as a pledge of peace; and no doubt he would have done so had not the inhabitants protested. Charles then surrendered the town of Pont Sainte-Maxence to Burgundy instead of Compiegne. But this sop did not at all satisfy the greedy Duke, whose mouth watered for Compiegne, which he was determined to obtain by fair or by foul means. At Soissons the Duke had succeeded in gaining the Governor by a bribe, and had, through this bribe, obtained the place; and there is little reason not to suppose that he was still more ready to offer a still greater bribe to obtain Compiegne. The Governor of Compiegne, William de Flavigny--a man very deeply suspected, writes Michelet of him--was not likely to refuse a bribe; and, as we shall see, he acted in a manner that has made the accusation of his treachery to his country and Joan of Arc almost a certainty.

It was to prevent, if possible, Compiegne falling into the hands of Burgundy that Joan of Arc hastened to its defence. On the 13th of May she reached Compiegne, where she was received with great joy by the citizens. The Maid lodged in the town with Mary le Boucher, wife of the ***Procureur*** of the King. At Compiegne were some important Court officials--the Chancellor Regnault de Chartres, no friend to Joan as we have seen, Vendome, and others. The country around and the places of armed strength were all in the occupation of the English and Burgundians; near Noyon, the town of Pont-l'Eveque was in the possession of the English. This place Joan of Arc attacked, and she was on the point of capturing it when a strong force of Burgundians arrived from Noyon, and Joan had to beat a retreat on Crecy. On the 23rd of May, news reached Joan that Compiegne was threatened by the united English and Burgundian forces, under the command of the Duke and the Earl of Arundel. By midnight of that day, Joan of Arc was back again in Compiegne. She had been warned of the danger of passing, to gain the town, through the enemies' lines with so small a company.

'Never fear!' she answered, 'we are enough. I must go and see my good friends at Compiegne.'

These words have been appropriately placed on the pedestal of the statue of the heroine in front of the Hotel de Ville in Compiegne.

By sunrise all her troopers were within the town: not a man was missing.

Compiegne was a strongly fortified place, resting on the left bank of the river Oise, across which, as at Orleans, one long stoutly defended bridge connected the right bank with the town. In front of the bridge was one of those redoubts which were in those days called 'boulevards.' This boulevard was surrounded by a wet moat or ditch connected with the principal bridge by a drawbridge, closed or opened from within at pleasure. The town was surrounded and protected by a broad and deep moat, filled from the river. Behind this moat rose the town walls, girt with strong towers at short intervals. On the right bank of the river extended a wide stretch of fertile meadow land, bounded on the northern horizon by the soft low-lying hills of Picardy. From the circuit of the walls across the plain the eye rested on the towns of Margny, of Clairvoix, and of Venette. The Burgundians were encamped at Margny and at Clairvoix; the English, under the command of Montgomery, were encamped at Venette.

The evening of the day on which she had arrived at Compiegne (the 24th of May), Joan of Arc resolved to attack the Burgundians, both at Margny and also at Clairvoix. Her plan was to draw out the Duke of Burgundy, should he come to the support of his men at these places. As to the English at Venette, she trusted that Flavy with his troops at Compiegne would prevent them from cutting her off after her attack on the Burgundians, and so intercepting her return to the town; but this unfortunately was the very disaster which occurred.

In front of the bridge the redoubts were filled by French archers to keep off any attack made by the English, and Flavy had placed a large number of boats filled with armed men, principally bowmen, in readiness along the river to receive their companions should they meet with a repulse in their attack on the Burgundians.

It was about five o'clock that afternoon when Joan of Arc rode out of Compiegne at the head of five hundred horsemen and foot soldiers. Flavy remained within the town, of which he was Governor. The attack led by the Maid on Margny, with splendid impetuosity, proved a complete success, and the enemy fled for shelter to their companions at Clairvoix. Here the resistance made was far more stubborn. While the French and Burgundians were combating in the meadows at Clairvoix, the English came from Venette to the assistance of their allies, and attacked the French in their rear. A panic was created by this attack among the French troops, and a ***sauve qui peut*** ensued, both foot and horse dashing back in confusion towards Compiegne, and when they reached the river either taking refuge in the boats or on the redoubts near the bridge. Mixed among this panic-stricken crowd of fugitives came the English in hot pursuit, followed by the Burgundians.

Carried away by the throng of frightened soldiers, Joan was among the last to leave the field, and to those who cried to her to make her escape she answered that all might yet be saved, and urged her men to rally. Nevertheless, she was forced back towards the bridge, across which fugitives were making their escape into the town. In a few seconds Joan could have been safe across the drawbridge, and under shelter of the towers which defended it. At this instant, whether intentionally to exclude the heroine from safety, or through panic and fear of the Burgundians and English entering the town along with the French, the drawbridge was lifted, and Joan, with a handful of the faithful few who were ever at her side in time of peril, was surrounded by a sea of foemen. In a moment half a dozen soldiers secured her horse and seized her on every side, trying to drag her out of the saddle. The long skirts which the heroine wore were soon torn off by these rough hands. An archer of Picardy, belonging to the army of John of Luxembourg, wrenched her from her horse and made her prisoner. Her brother Peter, her faithful squire d'Aulon, and Pothon de Xaintrailles were all captured at the same time.

Thus fell Joan of Arc into the hands of her enemies, and the question whether through treachery or not has never been settled.

According to an old work published early in the sixteenth century, called ***Le Miroir des Femmes Vertueuses***, Joan of Arc had taken the communion in the

Church of Saint James at Compiegne, and was standing leaning against a pillar of that church; a large number of citizens with many children stood around, to whom she said: 'My children and dear friends, I bid you to mark that I have been sold and betrayed, and that I shall be shortly put to death. So I beseech you all to pray to God for me, for never more shall I be able to be of service to the King or to the kingdom of France.'

This story, which, whether authentic or not, is surely a touching one, is full of the spirit of the heroine. It rests upon the testimony of two persons, one eighty-six and the other eighty-eight years of age, by whom the author was told the tale in 1498, both affirming that they had been in the church when Joan of Arc spoke of her betrayal. There can be but little doubt that Joan had had for some time before she went to Compiegne a presentiment of her soon falling into her enemies' power. On the eve of the King's coronation at Rheims she said to her friends that what she alone feared was treason--a foreboding too soon, alas! to come true. She never, however, seems to have fixed on any particular period when the treason she dreaded would occur; and during her trial she acknowledged that, had she known she would have been taken prisoner during the sortie on the 24th of May, she would not have undertaken that adventure.

One of her best historians, M. Wallon, thinks that the words which she is supposed to have spoken to the people in the Church of Saint James at Compiegne were owing to her discouragement at not having, a few weeks previously, been able to cross the river Aisne at Soissons, and thus finding herself prevented from attacking the Duke of Burgundy at Choisy, and thence having been obliged to return to Compiegne. Wallon points out that in coming to defend Compiegne, Joan of Arc came entirely at her own instigation, and that during the previous six months Flavy had defended Compiegne against the English and Burgundians with success and energy; nay more, that, in spite of bribes from the Duke of Burgundy, Flavy contrived to hold the town till the close of the war.

On the other side, a recent writer of the heroine's life, especially as regarded from a military standpoint, M. Marin, gives at great length his reasons for believing in the treachery of Flavy. M. Marin points out that, in the first place, Flavy's character was a notoriously bad one; secondly, that he was very possibly under the influence of both La Tremoille and the Chancellor Regnault de Chartres, bitter opponents, as we have already shown, of the Maid; thirdly, that it was in Flavy's interest that the prestige of saving Compiegne from the Burgundians and English should be entirely owing to his own conduct; and fourthly, that he, Flavy, with the majority of the French officers, was affected against Joan of Arc since the execution of Franquet d'Arras. M. Marin goes on to prove that Joan of Arc might have been rescued without difficulty, and that the enemy could not have forced their way into the town alongside of the retreating French, unless they were ready to be cut up as soon as they had come within its walls. M. Marin's opinion, having the authority of a soldier, carries weight with it; and his opinion is that Joan of Arc was deliberately betrayed by Flavy, and purposely allowed to fall into the hands of her enemies.

The names of La Tremoille and Regnault de Chartres should also be pilloried by the side of that of Flavy--the two great courtiers who held the ear of the King, and who had always plotted against Joan of Arc. As has already been said, it was Regnault de Chartres who had the effrontery to announce the news of Joan of Arc's capture to the citizens of Rheims as being a judgment of Heaven upon her. She had, this mean prelate said, offended God by her pride, and in wearing rich apparel, and in having preferred to follow her own will rather than that of God! Verily, and with reason, might poor Joan have prayed to be delivered from such friends as those creatures and courtiers about her King, for whom she had done and suffered so much.

* * * * *

The archer who had captured Joan of Arc was in the pay of the Bastard of Wandome, or Wandoune, and this Wandome was himself in the service of John de Ligny, a vassal of the Duke of Burgundy, and a cadet of the princely house of Luxembourg. Like most younger sons, John de Ligny was badly off, and the temptation of the English reward in exchange for his prisoner, whose escape he greatly feared, overtopped any scruples he may have felt in receiving this blood-money.

The historian Monstrelet tells us he was present when Joan of Arc was brought into the Burgundian camp, at Margny, and before the Duke of Burgundy. But the old chronicler relates nothing with regard to that eventful meeting; only he is eloquent on the joy caused by the capture of the Maid of Orleans among the English and their allies; and he tells us that in their opinion Joan's capture was equal by itself to that of five hundred ordinary prisoners, for they had feared her, he adds, more than all the other French leaders put together. Of the high opinion held by her enemies of the Maid's influence, one could not ask for a more remarkable proof than this testimony, coming as it does from a partisan of her foes.

After three days passed at Margny, Joan of Arc was taken, for greater security, by Luxembourg to the castle of Beaulieu, in Picardy.

CHAPTER V.
IMPRISONMENT AND TRIAL.

The news of Joan's capture soon reached Paris, and within a few hours of that event becoming known, the Vicar-General of the Order of the Inquisition sent a letter to the Duke of Burgundy, accompanied by another from the University of Paris, praying that Joan of Arc might be delivered up to the keeping of Mother Church as a sorceress and idolatress. That terrible engine, the Inquisition, had, like some mighty reptile scenting its prey near, slowly unfolded its coils. Whether Bedford had or had not caused these letters to be sent the Duke is not known, but the Regent had both in the Church and the University of Paris the men he wanted--instruments by whom his vengeance could be worked on Joan of Arc; and he had the astuteness to see that in calling in the aid of the Church, and treating Joan of Arc as a heretic and witch, the rules of war could be laid aside. What no civilised body of men could do, namely, kill a prisoner of war, that thing could be done in the name and by the authority of the Church and its holy office; and in the Bishop of Beauvais, the inexorable Cauchon, Bedford had the tool necessary to his hand whereby this dastardly plot could be carried out.

The first move that Bedford now was obliged to take was to secure the victim; and in order to do so the Bishop of Beauvais was applied to. The name of Peter Cauchon, Bishop of Beauvais, will go down to the latest posterity with the execration of humanity, for the part he played in the tragedy of the worst of judicial murders of which any record exists. Let us give even the devil his due. According to Michelet the Bishop was 'not a man without merit,' although the historian does not say in what Cauchon's merit consisted. Born at Rheims, he had been considered a learned priest when at the University of Paris; but he had the reputation of being a harsh and vindictive opponent to all who disagreed with his views, within or without the Church. He was forced to leave Paris, in 1413, for some misconduct. It was then that Cauchon became a strong partisan of the Duke of Burgundy. It was through the Duke that he obtained the See of Beauvais. The English also favoured Cauchon, and obtained for him a high post in the University of Paris. When the tide of French success reached Beauvais, in 1429, Cauchon was obliged to escape, and found shelter in England. There Winchester received him with cordiality. While in England, Cauchon became a thorough partisan of the English, and the humble servant of the proud Prince-Cardinal. Winchester promised Cauchon preferment, and, when the See of Rouen fell vacant, recommended the Pope to place Cauchon on its throne. The Pope, however, refused his consent, and the Rouen Chapters would hear naught of the Anglicised Bishop. At that time the Church at Rouen was at war with the University of Paris, and did not wish one of the members of that University placed over it.

Joan of Arc's place of capture happened to be in the diocese of Beauvais, and although Cauchon was now only nominally Bishop of Beauvais, he still retained that title. Cauchon now placed himself, body and soul, at the disposal of the English, hoping thereby sooner to obtain the long-coveted Archbishopric of Rouen in exchange for helping his friends to the utmost in his power by furthering their schemes and in ridding them of their prisoner once and for ever. The bait held out by Winchester and Bedford was the Archbishopric of Rouen, and eagerly did Cauchon seize his prey. What added to his zeal was his wish to gratify base feelings of revenge on those who had thrust him out of his Bishopric of Beauvais, and on her without whose deeds he might have still been living in security in his palatial home there.

After a consultation with the leaders of the University of Paris, Cauchon arrived at the Burgundian camp before Compiegne on the 14th of July, and claimed Joan of Arc as prisoner from the keeping of the Duke of Burgundy. Cauchon justified his demand by letters which he had obtained from the doctors of the University, and he made the offer in the name of the child-king of England. The sum handed over for the purchase of the prisoner was 10,000 livres tournois, equivalent to 61,125 francs of French money of to-day--about L2400 sterling. This was the ordinary price in that day for the ransom of any prisoner of high rank. Luxembourg, to his shame and that of his order, consented to the sale on those terms, and Cauchon soon returned with the news of his bargain to his English employers.

The whole transaction sounds more like what one might expect to have occurred amongst an uncivilised nation rather than among a people who prided themselves on their chivalry and their usages of fair-play in matters relating to warfare. That a high dignitary of the Church, and a countryman of Joan of Arc, should have bought her from a prince, the descendant of emperors and kings, also a countryman of the heroic Maid's, for English gold, is bad enough; and that the so-called 'good' Duke of Burgundy should have been a silent spectator of the infamous transaction, brands all the actors as among the most sordid and meanest of individuals. But what is infinitely worse is the fact that no steps appear to have been taken by Charles to rescue the Maid, or to attempt an exchange of her for any other prisoner or prisoners.

Thus Joan of Arc, bound literally hand and foot, was led like a lamb to the shambles, not a hand being raised by those for whom she had done such great and noble deeds.

The University of Paris, whose decisions carried so great a weight in the issue of the trial of the Maid of Orleans, consisted at this period of an ecclesiastical body of doctors; but as far as its attributes consisted it was a body secular, and holding an independent position owing to its many privileges. The University was a political as well as an ecclesiastical body, supreme under the Pope above the whole of the Gallican Church. Although divided into two parties through the war then raging between England and France, its judicature was greatly influenced by the Church. It was a matter of certainty that the Doctors of Theology who sat in the University of Paris, and who were all, or nearly all, French by birth, would favour the English, and give an adverse decision to that of those French ecclesiastics who had examined into Joan's life and character when assembled at Poitiers, and who then considered her to be acting under the influence and with the protection of the Almighty.

As a prisoner, Joan of Arc's behaviour was as modest and courageous as it had been in her days of success and liberty. In the first times of her durance, d'Aulon, who, as we mentioned, had been captured at the same time, appears to have been allowed to remain with her. On his telling her that he feared Compiegne would now probably be taken by the enemy, Joan of Arc said such a thing could not occur, 'For all the places,' she added, 'which the King of Heaven has placed in the keeping of King Charles by my means will never again be retaken by his enemies, at any rate as long as he cares to keep them.'

Although willing to endure for the sake of her beloved country all the cruelty her enemies could inflict upon her, Joan was most anxious to return in order to continue her mission. While in the castle of Beaulieu she made a desperate attempt to escape. She managed to squeeze herself between two beams of wood placed across an opening in her prison, and was on the point of leaving her dungeon tower when one of the jailers caught sight of her, and she was retaken. Probably in consequence of this attempt, Joan of Arc, after an imprisonment of four months at Beaulieu, was transferred thence by Ligny to his castle of Beaurevoir, near the town of Cambrai, a place far removed from the neighbourhood of the war, and consequently more secure than Beaulieu. At Beaurevoir lived the wife and the aunt of Ligny; they showed some attention and compassion to the prisoner. They offered her some of their dresses, and tried to persuade her to quit her male attire. Joan, however, refused: she gave as her reason for not complying with their request that the time had not yet arrived for her to cease wearing the clothes she had worn during the time of her mission. That she had good reason not to don woman's attire even when at Beaurevoir, and keep to her male attire as a protection, is probable, as she was not safe from wanton insult at the hands of the rough soldiery placed about her person. This clinging to her male dress, we shall see, under similar circumstances at Rouen, was the principal indictment made against her by her executioners.

At Beaurevoir Joan of Arc was placed in a chamber at the top of a high tower, whence Ligny thought that no attempt at escape would be made, but Joan of Arc tried once again to recover her liberty. In the course of her trial she told her judges how her voices counselled her not again to make this venture, and of her perplexity whether she should obey them, or, at the risk of her life, escape from the clutches of the English, for at this time she knew that she had been sold to her bitterest foes.

What appears to have determined her decision was hearing that Compiegne was in imminent peril of falling into the hands of the English, and that the inhabitants would be massacred. In her desperation, feeling, like young Arthur, that

> 'The wall is high; and yet will I leap down:--
> Good ground, be pitiful, and hurt me not!...

As good to die, and go, as die, and stay'

she knotted some thongs together and let herself out of a window; but the thongs broke, and she fell from a great height--the tower is supposed to have been no less than sixty feet high. She was found unconscious at its foot, and for several days she was not expected to recover from the injuries she had received. But she was doomed for a far more terrible death.

For several days Joan of Arc took no nourishment. Gradually she revived, and she told her jailers that her beloved Saint Catherine had visited and comforted her; and she also told them that she knew Compiegne would not be taken, and would be free from its enemies before the Feast of Saint Martin.

Beaurevoir is now a ruin: although above the lintel can still be seen the coat-of-arms of the jailer of the Maid, the tower in which she was imprisoned, and from which she so nearly met her death, has been destroyed.

In the month of November of that year (1430), in spite of the entreaties of his wife and aunt, Ligny delivered up his prisoner into the custody of the Duke of Burgundy, from whose keeping she was soon transferred into that of the English.

On the 20th of November the University of Paris sent a message to Cauchon, advising him to bring Joan of Arc before a tribunal. Cauchon, however, waited the arrival of Winchester, bringing with him his great-nephew, Henry VI. Winchester arrived with the boy-king on the 2nd of December. The Cardinal intended the function of the crowning of his great-nephew to be as imposing a ceremony as possible; and he also meant, by defaming the source of the French King's successes, to show the French people that Charles' coronation at Rheims had been brought about by what the Regent Bedford called a 'limb of the evil one.' It was, therefore, Bedford's plan that it should be declared before the world that Joan of Arc was inspired by Satanic agencies, and that consequently the French King's coronation was also due to these agencies. By similar means it would be made clear that all the French victories were owing to the same influence; for were it not, argued the English, they would be proved to have been themselves fighting against and defeated by--not the spirit of evil but--the spirit of righteousness.

Nothing, indeed, could be clearer than Winchester's argument. It was now only necessary that Joan of Arc should be at once placed on her trial as a sorceress and a witch--one who was in league with the evil one; and, when that had been satisfactorily proved, that she should publicly meet with the fate which a merciful Church had, in its infinite wisdom, ordained for such as she. Thus would the English army and people be avenged, and the French King's crown and prerogative suffer an irreparable damage.

From Beaurevoir, Joan of Arc was first taken to the town of Arras, thence to Crotoy, where, about the 21st of November, she was handed over to the English.

A chronicler of that day writes that the English rejoiced as greatly on that occasion as if they had received all the wealth of Lombardy. The Duke of Burgundy had never merited the title of 'Good,' which, somehow or other, has been linked with his name. Had he been the most virtuous of princes of any time, he yet deserves to have his memory branded for the part he then took in the sale of Joan of Arc--a transaction whereof the poor excuse of not losing the benefits of his alliance with the English avails nothing. For this, if nothing else, we reverse the good fame which lying history has accorded him.

In the underground portion of a tower at Crotoy, still to be seen, although the upper part has disappeared, facing the sea, is a door-way, which local tradition points out as that of the dungeon of Joan of Arc. Crotoy, or Le Crotoy, is on the coast of Picardy, a little to the north of Abbeville. In the fifteenth century it was a place of some warlike importance, especially to the English. Its situation near the coast, and the strength of its fortress, made Le Crotoy one of the principal places on the sea line, whence stores and war provender could be carried into France. Le Crotoy had fallen into possession of the English through the marriage of Henry III. with Eleanor of Castille, Countess of Ponthieu, of which Crotoy formed a part. During the hundred years' war, the port could receive vessels of considerable tonnage; and from this point the booty taken by the English could be shipped and sent across the Channel. Now but a few vestiges can be traced of its once strong and ably fortified castle. A few years ago, a statue, representing the Maid of Orleans in the garb of a prisoner, was placed near the ruins of the castle in which she passed most of the month of December, 1430.

At Crotoy, Joan of Arc was permitted to assist at the celebration of the Mass in the chapel of the castle; and while here she received a visit from some of her admirers from Abbeville--a few noble hearts who still remained loyal to the once all-powerful deliveress of their country, now a poor and abandoned prisoner on her road to a long imprisonment and a cruel death! Touched by this mark of sympathy from these Abbeville folk, Joan gave them, on parting from them, her blessing, and asked them to remember her in their prayers. The enlightened clergy and doctors, lay and spiritual, who formed the body known as the University of Paris, preferred that Joan of Arc should be sent to the capital, there to undergo her trial, and wrote to this effect to Bedford, through the name of the boy-king. They also despatched a letter to Cauchon (probably inspired by Bedford), in which they rated him for not bringing the Maid at once to her trial. They told him he was showing a lamentable laxness in not immediately punishing the scandals which had been committed under his jurisdiction against the Christian religion.

Paris was not considered enough of a safe place to take Joan of Arc into; the French lay too near its walls, and the loyalty of its citizens to the English was a doubtful quantity. Besides, it was not convenient that the University of Paris should be allowed the entire direction of the trial. It was well that the University should be made use of; but Cauchon relied on the Inquisition to carry out his and Bedford's plan. Cauchon must be the principal agent and judge, and he felt, with Bedford, that they had a freer hand if the trial were to be at Rouen; therefore Rouen was decided on as the place of trial and punishment. Rouen, also, being in the midst of the English possessions, was perfectly safe from attack, should it occur to any of Joan of Arc's countrymen to attempt a rescue.

At the close of December Joan of Arc was taken across the river Somme, in a boat, to Saint Valery, and thence, strongly guarded, and placed on horseback, she was led along the Normandy coast by Eure and Dieppe to the place of her martyrdom. On arriving at Rouen it was seriously debated by some of her captors whether or not she should be at once put to death. They suggested her being sewn into a sack and thrown into the river! The reason these people gave for summarily disposing of Joan of Arc without form or trial was that, as long as she lived, there was no security for the English in France. As has already been noticed, those who commanded and sided with the English were desirous that Joan of Arc should be first branded as a witch and a sorceress, both by the doctors of the Church and by the State, before being put to death.

Arrived at Rouen, Joan of Arc was immured in the old fortress built by Philip

Augustus. One tower alone remains of the seven massive round towers which surrounded the circular castle. Her jailers had the barbarity to place their prisoner in an iron cage, in which she was fastened with iron rings and chains, one at the neck, another at the hands, and a third confining the feet. Joan was thus caged as if she were a wild animal until her trial commenced. After that, she was chained to a miserable truckle bed.

A chronicler of that time, named Macy, tells the following story of an incident which, for the sake of English manhood, one trusts is untrue. Among others who went to see Joan of Arc in her prison came one day the Earl of Warwick, with Lord Stafford and Ligny--Joan's former jailer. The latter told her in a jeering way that he had come to buy her back from the English, provided she promised never again to make war against them.

'You are mocking me,' said Joan of Arc. 'For I know that you have not the power to do that, neither the will.' And she added, 'I know well that these English will kill me, thinking that by doing so they will reconquer the kingdom of France; but even if there were one hundred thousand Godons more in France than there are now, they will never again conquer the kingdom!'

On hearing these words Stafford drew his dagger, and would have struck her had not Warwick prevented the cowardly act.

Cauchon formed his tribunal of the following:--

1. John Graverent, a Dominican priest, D.D., Grand Inquisitor of France. It was he who appointed John Lemaitre as judge in the trial of the Maid. The following July this Graverent preached a sermon in Paris, in which he glorified the death of Joan of Arc.

2. John Lemaitre, who represented the Inquisition on the trial. He was a Dominican prior. He appears to have been a feeble-minded creature, and a mere tool of Cauchon and Graverent.

3. Martin Bellarme, D.D., another Dominican, and also a member of the Inquisition.

4. John d'Estivet, surnamed 'Benedicite,' canon of Beauvais and Bayeux, was another of Cauchon's creatures. He acted the part of ***Procureur-General*** during the trial. D'Estivet was a gross and cruel ecclesiastic, and it is somewhat satisfactory to know his end. He was found dead in a muddy ditch soon after Joan of Arc's death.

As M. Fabre justly says, 'He perished in his native element.'

5. John de la Fontaine, M.A. He was **_Conseille d'Instruction_** during the trial. In the course of it he was threatened by Cauchon for having given some friendly advice to the prisoner, and escaped from Rouen before the conclusion of the trial.

6, 7, 8. William Manchon, William Colles, and Nicolas Taquel, all three recorders. They belonged to the Church. It is to Manchon that we are indebted for a summary of the most interesting account of the trial. We shall find that at the time of Joan's execution this man was horrified at the part he had taken in it. He confesses his horror at having received money for his infamy, but instead of casting his blood-money at the feet of Cauchon, and hanging himself like another Judas, he somewhat naively informs us that he laid it out in the purchase of a breviary in order to pray for the soul of the martyr.

9. Massieu, another priest, who acted as the sheriffs officer. He appears to have had feelings of humanity, and attended Joan to the end.

10. Louis de Luxembourg, Bishop of Therouenne and the Chancellor of France to King Henry VI. This bishop was the go-between of Cauchon and Winchester throughout the trial; but he only appears to have taken part in these occasions during the examinations. It was he who was made Archbishop of Rouen, which post Cauchon had hoped to gain; and it was for this archbishopric that Cauchon had taken the presiding post during the trial.

11. John de Mailly, Bishop of Noyon; he was another staunch auxiliary of Cauchon. In the year 1456, at the trial for the rehabilitation of Joan of Arc's memory, Mailly signed his name among those who condemned the deed he had helped to carry out.

12. Zanon de Castiglione, Bishop of Lisieux. One of the reasons that this man gave for condemning Joan of Arc to the stake was that she was born in too low a rank of life to have been inspired by God. This decision makes one wonder so aristocratic a prelate could demean himself by belonging to a religion which owed its origin to One who had followed the trade of a carpenter.

13. Philibert de Montjeu, Bishop of Coutances.

14. John de Saint Avet, Bishop of Avranches. The latter was the only one of the above Bishops, Dominicans, and members of the French Church who gave his vote against the condemnation of Joan of Arc, although the trial minutes have not

recorded the fact.

Besides the above French prelates, were:--

15. John Beaupere, M.A. and D.D., formerly a rector of the University of Paris, also a canon of Besancon. It was he who, with the following five representatives of the University of Paris, took the most prominent part in the cross-questioning of the prisoner.

16. Thomas de Courcelles, a canon of Amiens, of Therouenne, and of Laon. This person was employed to read the articles of accusation to the prisoner, and was in favour of employing torture to make Joan confess what was required of her by her prosecutors. He was considered one of the shining lights of the University of Paris. He died in 1469, and until the Revolution an engraved slab, on which his virtues and learning were recorded, covered his remains.

17. Gerard Feuillet. He was sent to Paris during the trial in order to lay the twelve articles of accusation before the University, and did not take part in the latter portion of the trial.

18. Nicolas Midi, D.D., a celebrated preacher. He is supposed to have been the author of the twelve articles; and he it was who preached a sermon at the time of the execution of Joan of Arc. Attacked soon after by leprosy, he sufficiently recovered to see Charles VII. enter Paris; and he had the audacity to send the King an address of felicitation in the name of the faculties of the University by whose instrumentality Joan of Arc had been executed.

19. Peter Morice, a doctor of the University and a canon of Rouen. He was one of the most eager to bring Joan to the stake.

20. James de Touraine, also a doctor of the University, was violently hostile to Joan of Arc.

The above six doctors, with Cauchon, were those who had most to do with the proceedings of the trial, and those whose duty it was principally to question the prisoner.

21. Nicolas Loiseleur, M.A., a canon of Rouen; he was the most abject of all the gang of priests and doctors who formed part of this infamous tribunal. It was Loiseleur who, in the disguise of a layman, attempted to worm secrets from Joan, pretending to be her friend and sympathiser. When he found he gained nothing by the subterfuge, he resumed his clerical garb, and succeeded in getting, under

the promise of secrecy from his order, a confession from the prisoner. He also introduced spies into the prison who took notes of Joan's words. When the idea was mooted of putting Joan of Arc to the torture, Loiseleur was one of the most urgent for it to be applied. However, on the day of the execution this man, who, strange as it may seem, appears to have had some kind of conscience, or at least to have been able to feel remorse for the base part he had played in the trial of the Maid, implored Joan of Arc's forgiveness. He, however, after the execution, helped Cauchon to spread calumnies regarding their victim. This infamous scoundrel died suddenly at Basle.

22. Raoul Roussel de Vernon, D.C.L., and the canon treasurer of the Cathedral of Rouen. He acted throughout the trial as reporter. In 1443 Roussel became Archbishop of Rouen.

23. Robert Barbier, also a D.C.L., and canon of Rouen Cathedral.

24. Nicolas Coppequesne, also a canon of Rouen Cathedral.

25. Nicolas de Venderes, a canon of Rouen, and Cauchon's chaplain.

26. John Alessee, also a canon of Rouen. This Alessee was greatly moved at the heroine's death, and exclaimed, 'I pray to God my soul may one day be where hers is now.'

27. Raoul Auguy, another canon.

28. William de Baubribosc, also a canon of Rouen.

29. John Brullot, another canon and precentor of Rouen.

30. John Basset, another canon and a M.A.

31. John Brullot, another canon. Besides these were seventeen others, named Caval, Columbel, Cormeilles, Crotoy, Duchemin, Dubesert, Garin, Gastinel, Ledoux, Leroy, Maguerie, Manzier, Morel, Morellet, Pinchon, Saulx, and Pasquier de Vaux, who became Bishop of Meaux, Evreux, and Lisieux. In all, nine-and-twenty canons of Rouen.

After these came a list of mitred abbots, priors, and heads of religious houses: Peter de Crique, Prior of Sigy; William Lebourg, Prior of the College of Saint Lo of Rouen; Peter Migiet, Prior of Longueville.

After these priors came eleven abbots: Durement, Abbot of Fecamp, later Bishop of Coutances; Benel, Abbot of Courcelles; De Conti, Abbot of Sainte Catherine; Dacier, Abbot of Saint Corneille of Compiegne; Frique, Abbot of Bee; Jolivet, Abbot of Saint Michael's Mount in Normandy; Labbe, Abbot of Saint George de Bocherville; Leroux, Abbot of Jumieges; Du Masle, Abbot of Saint Ouen; Moret, Abbot of Preaux; and Theroude, Abbot of Mortemer.

Besides these there were many doctors and assessors from the University of Paris; among the latter lot appears the name of an English priest, William Haiton, a secretary of Henry VI. He and William Alnwick, Bishop of Norwich, Privy Seal to the English King, are the only two names belonging to the English clergy who took part in the trial. The Cardinal of Winchester never once appeared during the proceedings, although he was, together with Cauchon, the prime mover in the business. To complete the list of the other French clergy--French only by birth and nationality indeed--must be added the names of Chatillon, Archdeacon of Evreux; Erard, Canon of Langres, Laon, and Beauvais; Martin Ladvenu, a Dominican priest, one of the few who showed some humanity to the prisoner. It was Ladvenu who heard her confession on the day of her execution, and who after her death testified to her saintliness. Isambard de la Pierre, also a Dominican. Although he voted for her death, de la Pierre showed signs of pity and compassion for his victim, and assisted her at her last moments. Testimony to her pure character was given by him in the time of her rehabilitation. Besides these were Emenyart, Fiexvet, Guerdon, Le Fevre, Delachambre, and Tiphanie, all of whom, with the exception of the last two, who were doctors of medicine, were members of the University. As we have already stated, out of this vast crowd of ecclesiastics and a few laymen, only two Englishmen took part in the trial. But the immediate guard of the prisoner was composed of English soldiers--namely, of the following: John Gris, an English knight, one of Henry's bodyguard, who was in personal attendance on Joan of Arc; also John Berwoit (?) and William Talbot, subordinator to Gris. These men commanded a set of soldiers called *houspilleurs*, placed in the cell of the prisoner day and night. According to J. Bellow's pocket dictionary, the term *houspilleur* is derived from the old French term *houspiller*--Ang. 'to worry.' And these fellows certainly carried out that meaning of the word.

If anything is needed to prove what an important case the English and those allied to them in France considered that of Joan of Arc, the great number of prelates and doctors assembled to judge her is sufficient to show. The doctors who had been summoned to attend the trial, and who had come to Rouen from Paris, were well paid by Winchester. Some of the receipts are still in existence. The Inquisition and Cauchon also received pay from the English Government.

Besides money, as we have said, Cauchon expected also to receive the Archbishopric of Rouen for his zeal in bringing Joan of Arc to the stake. Cupidity, lust of place and power, and fear of the enemies of the French were the principal motives which influenced these men, whose names should for ever be execrated. In truth, a vulgar greed induced them to destroy one of the noblest creatures that had ever honoured humanity.

The ***proces-verbal*** and the minutes of the trial were written in Latin, and translated by Thomas de Courcelles; only a portion of the original translation has been preserved. There were three reporters who took notes during the trial--Manchon, Colles, and Taquel. The notes in Latin, written as the trial proceeded, were collected in the evenings, and translated into French by Manchon.

One difficult question arises--namely, are these notes to be relied on? Manchon appears to have been honest in his writing, but Cauchon was not to be trifled with in what he wished noted, as the following instance will show. A sheriff's officer, named Massieu, was overheard to say that Joan of Arc had done nothing worthy of the death sentence. It was repeated to Cauchon, who threatened to have Massieu drowned. When Isambert de la Pierre advised Joan to submit herself to the Council then holding meetings at Bale, to which she assented, Cauchon shouted out, 'In the devil's name hold your peace!' On being asked by Manchon whether the prisoner's wish to submit her case to the Council at Bale should be placed on the minutes of the trial, Cauchon roughly refused. Joan of Arc overhearing this, said, 'You write down what is against my interest, but not what is in my favour.' But we think the truth comes out, on the whole, pretty clearly; and we have in the answers of Joan to her judges, however much these answers may have been altered to suit Cauchon's views and ultimate object, a splendid proof of her presence of mind and courage. This she maintained day after day in the face of that crowd of enemies who left no stone unturned, no subtlety of law or superstition disused, to bring a charge of guilt against her.

No victory of arms that Joan of Arc might have accomplished, had her career continued one bright and unclouded success, could have shown in a grander way the greatness of her character than her answers and her bearing during the entire course of her examinations before her implacable enemies, her judicial murderers.

After holding some preliminary and private meetings, in which Cauchon, with some of the prelates, drew up a series of articles of indictment against the prisoner, the first public sitting of the tribunal took place in the chapel of the castle, in the same building in which Joan was imprisoned.

This was on the 21st of February, 1431. As we have said, from the day of her arrival in Rouen, at the end of December of the previous year, till this 21st day of February, Joan had been kept in an iron cage--a martyrdom of fifty days' daily and nightly torture. During the trial her confinement was less barbarous, but she was kept chained to a wooden bed, and the only wonder is that she did not succumb to this barbarous imprisonment. We shall see that she fell seriously ill, and the English at one time feared she would die a natural death, and defeat their object of having her exposed and destroyed as a witch and a heretic.

On the day before the meeting of the tribunal, Cauchon sent summonses for all the judges to attend. Joan of Arc had meanwhile made two demands, both of which were refused. One was, that an equal number of clergy belonging to the French party should form an equal number in the tribunal to those of the English faction. The other demand was that she should be allowed to hear Mass before appearing before the tribunal.

At eight in the morning of Wednesday, the 21st of February, Cauchon took his seat as presiding judge for the trial about to commence. Beneath him were ranged forty-three assessors--there were ninety-five assessors in all who took part in the trial. On the public days their numbers varied from between forty to sixty.

The prisoner was led into the chapel by the priest Massieu. Cauchon opened the proceedings with the following harangue:--

'This woman,' he said, pointing to Joan of Arc, 'this woman has been seized and apprehended some time back, in the territory of our diocese of Beauvais. Numerous acts injurious to the orthodox faith have been committed by her, not merely in our diocese, but in many other regions. The public voice which accuses her of such crimes has become known throughout Christendom, and quite recently the high and very Christian Prince, our lord the King, has delivered her up and given her in our custody in order that a trial in the cause of religion shall be made, as it seemeth right and proper. For as much in the eyes of public opinion, and owing to certain matters which have come to our knowledge'--(Cauchon here refers to the information that he sought to obtain from Domremy: as nothing could be learnt there but what redounded to Joan of Arc's credit, no further use was made of the information by the Bishop)--'we have, with the assistance of learned doctors in religious and civil law, called you together in order to examine the said Joan, in order that she be examined on matters relating to faith. Therefore,' he continued, 'we desire in this trial that you fill the duty of your office for the preservation and exaltation of the Catholic faith; and, with the Divine assistance of our Lord, we call upon you to expedite these proceedings for the welfare of your consciences, that you speak the plain and honest truth, without subterfuge or concealment, on all questions that will be made you touching the faith. And in the first place we call upon you to take the oath in the form prescribed. Swear, the hands placed on the Gospels, that you will answer the truth in the questions that will be asked you.'

The latter words the Bishop had addressed to Joan; who answered that she knew not on what Cauchon would question her. 'Perhaps,' she said, 'you will ask me things about which I cannot answer you.'

'Will you swear,' said Cauchon, 'to tell the truth respecting the things which will be asked you concerning the faith, and of which you are cognisant?'

'Of all things regarding my family, and what things I have done since coming into France, I will gladly answer; but, as regards the revelation which I have received from God, I have never revealed to any one, except to Charles my King, and I will never reveal these things, even if my head were to be cut off, because my voices have ordered me not to confide these things to any one save the King. But,' she continued, 'in eight days' time I shall know whether or not I may be allowed to tell you about them.'

Cauchon then repeated his question to the prisoner, namely, whether she would answer any questions put to her regarding matters of faith, and the Gospels were placed before her. The prisoner, kneeling, laid her hands upon them, and swore to speak the truth in what was asked her as regarded matters of faith.

'What is your name?' asked Cauchon.

J.--'In my home I was called Jeannette. Since I came to France I was called Joan. I have no surname.'

C.--'Where were you born?'

J.--'At Domremy, near Greux. The principal church is at Greux.'
C.--'What are your parents' names?'
J.--'My father's name is James d'Arc; my mother's, Isabella.'
C.--'Where were you baptized?'
J.--'At Domremy.'

Cauchon then asked her the names of her god-parents, who baptized her, her age (she was about nineteen), and what her education amounted to.

'I have learnt,' Joan said, in answer to the last question, 'from my mother the Paternoster, the Ave Maria, and the Belief. All that I know has been taught me by my mother.'

Cauchon then called upon her to repeat the Lord's Prayer.

In trials for heresy the prisoners had to repeat this prayer before the judges. At the commencement of Joan of Arc's trial the crime of magic was brought against her, but as Cauchon completely failed to find any evidence for such a charge against his prisoner, he altered the charge of magic into one of heresy. It was probably supposed that a heretic would be unable to repeat the prayer and the creed, being under diabolic influence.

Joan of Arc then asked whether she might make her confession before the tribunal. Cauchon refused this request, but told her that he would send some one to whom she might confess. He then warned her that if she were to leave her prison she would be condemned as a heretic. Considering the way she was chained to her cell, it sounds strange that Cauchon should fear her flight.

'I have never,' the Maid said, 'given my promise not to attempt to escape if I can.'

'Have you anything to complain about?' asked the Bishop; and Joan then said how cruelly she was fastened by chains round her body and her feet. Probably, had she then promised not to escape from prison, this severity would have been relaxed, but Joan of Arc had not the spirit to stoop to her persecutors; she would not give her word not to get free if she could. 'The hope of escape is allowed to every prisoner,' she bravely said.

At the close of the sitting, John Gris, the English knight who had the chief charge over the prisoner, with the two soldiers Berwoit and Talbot, were called, and took an oath not to allow the prisoner to see any one without Cauchon's permission, and to strictly guard the prisoner. And with that the first day's trial ended.

Manchon, in his minutes on the day's proceedings, says that shouts and interruptions interfered with the reporters and their notes, and that Joan of Arc was repeatedly interrupted. Cauchon had placed some of his clerks behind the tapestry in the depth of a window of the chapel, whose duty it was to make a garbled copy of Joan of Arc's answers to suit the Bishop.

Possibly finding the chapel of the castle too small for the number of people present at the trial, the next meeting of the judges was held in a different place, more suitable--namely, in the great hall of the castle. That second day's trial took place on the 22nd of February. The tribunal consisted of Cauchon and forty-seven assessors.

Cauchon commenced the proceedings by introducing John Lemaitre, vicar of the Inquisition, to the judges, after which Joan was brought into the hall--a splendid chamber used on happier occasions for festivities and Court pageants.

Cauchon again commanded the prisoner to take the oath, as on the first day's trial. She said that she had already once sworn to speak nothing but the truth, and that that should suffice. Cauchon still insisted, and again Joan replied that as far as any question was put to her regarding faith and religion she had promised to answer, but that she could not promise more, and Cauchon failed to get anything more from her.

The Bishop then applied to one of the doctors of theology to examine and cross-question the prisoner. This man's name was Beaupere.

B.--'In the first place, Joan, I will exhort you to tell the truth, as you have sworn to do, on all that I may have to ask you.'

J.--'You may ask me questions on which I shall be able to answer you, and on others about which I cannot. If you were well informed about me you should wish me out of your power. All that I have done has been the work of revelation.'

B.--'How old were you when you left your home?'

J.--'I do not exactly know.'

B.--'Did you learn any trade at home?'

J.--'Yes, to sew and to spin, and for that I am not afraid to be matched by any woman in Rouen?'

B.--'Did you not once leave your father's house before you left it altogether?'

J.--'We left for fear of the Burgundians, and I once left my father's house and went to Neufchateau in Lorraine, to visit a woman named La Rousse, where I remained for fifteen days.'

B.--'What was your occupation when at home?'

J.--'When I was with my father I looked after the household affairs, and I went but seldom with the sheep and cattle to the fields.'

B.--'Did you make your confession every year?'

J.--'Yes, to my curate, and when he was prevented hearing it, to another priest, with my curate's permission. I think on two or three occasions I have confessed to mendicant friars. That happened at Neufchateau. I took the Communion at Easter.'

B.--'Have you received the Eucharist at other festivals besides that of Easter?'

Joan of Arc said that what she had already told regarding this question was sufficient.

'Passez outre' is the term she used, not an easy one to translate. Perhaps 'that will suffice' is like it.

Beaupere now began questioning Joan of Arc regarding 'her voices,' and one can imagine how eagerly this portion of the prisoner's examination must have been listened to by all present.

'When did you first hear the voices?' asked Beaupere.

'I was thirteen,' answered Joan, 'when I first heard a voice coming from God to help me to live well. That first time I was much alarmed. The voice came to me about mid-day; it was in the summer, and I was in my father's garden.'

'Had you been fasting?' asked Beaupere.

J.--'Yes, I had been fasting.'

B.--'Had you fasted on the day before?'

J.--'No, I had not.'

B.--'From what direction did the voices come?'

J.--'I heard the voice coming from my right--from towards the church.'

B.--'Was the voice accompanied with a bright light?'

J.--'Seldom did I hear it without seeing a bright light. The light came from the same side as did the voice, and it was generally very brilliant. When I came into France I often heard the voices very loud.'

B.--'How could you see the light when you say it was at the side?'

To this question Joan gave no direct answer, but she said that when she was in a wood she would hear the voices coming towards her.

'What,' next asked Beaupere, 'what did you think this voice which manifested itself to you sounded like?'

J.--'It seemed to me a very noble voice, and I think it was sent to me by God. When I heard it for the third time I recognised it as being the voice of an angel.'

B.--'Could you understand it?'

J.--'It was always quite clear, and I could easily understand it.'

B.--'What advice did it give you regarding the salvation of your soul?'

J.--'It told me to conduct myself well, and to attend the services of the Church regularly; and it told me that it was necessary that I should go to France.'

B.--'In what manner of form did the voice appear?'

J.--'As to that I will give you no answer.'

B.--'Did that voice solicit you often?'

J.--'It said to me two or three times a week, "Leave your village and go to France."'

B.--'Did your father know of your departure?'

J.--'He knew nothing about it. The voice said, "Go to France," so I could not remain at home any longer.'

B.--'What else did it say to you?'

J.--'It told me that I should raise the siege of Orleans.'

B.--'Was that all?'

J.--'The same voice told me to go to Vaucouleurs, to Robert de Baudricourt, captain of that place, and that he would give me soldiers to accompany me on my journey; and I answered it, that I was a poor girl who did not know how to ride, neither how to fight.'

B.--'What did you do then?'

J.--'I went to my uncle, and told him that I wished to remain with him for some time, and I lived with him eight days. I then told him that I must go to Vaucouleurs, and he took me there. When I arrived there I recognised Robert de Baudricourt, although it was the first time that I saw him.'

B.--'How, then, did you recognise him?'

J.--'I knew him through my voices. They said to me, "This is the man," and I said to him, "I must go to France." Twice he refused to listen to me. The third time he received me. The voices had told me this would happen.'

B.--'Had you not some business with the Duke of Lorraine?'

J.--'The Duke ordered that I should be brought to him. I went and said to him, "I must go to France." The Duke asked me how he should recover his health. I told him I knew nothing about that.'

B.--'Did you speak much to him about your journey?'

J.--'I told him very little about it. But I asked him to allow his son, with some soldiers, to go to France with me, and that I should pray God to cure him. I had gone to him with a safe conduct. After leaving him I returned to Vaucouleurs.'

B.--'How were you dressed when you left Vaucouleurs?'

J.--'When I left Vaucouleurs I wore a man's dress. I had on a sword which Robert de Baudricourt had given me, without any other arms. I was accompanied by a knight, a squire, and four servants. We went to the town of Saint Urban, and I passed that night in the abbey. On the way, we passed through the town of Auxerre, where I attended mass in the principal church. At that time I heard my voices often, with that one of which I have already spoken.'

B.--'Tell me, now, by whose advice did you come to wear the dress of a man?'

Joan of Arc refused to answer, in spite of being repeatedly told to do so.

B.--'What did Baudricourt say to you when you left?'

J.--'He made them who went with me promise to take charge of me, and as I left he said, "Go, and let come what may!"' (Advienne que pourra!)

B.--'What do you know regarding the Duke of Orleans, now a prisoner in England?'

J.--'I know that God protects the Duke of Orleans, and I have had more revelations about the Duke than about any other person in the world, with the exception of the King.'

She was now again asked as to who it was who had advised her to wear male attire. She said it was necessary that she should dress in that manner.

'Did your voice tell you so?' was asked her.

'I believe my voice gave me good advice,' she answered.

B.--'What did you do on arriving at Orleans?'

J.--'I sent a letter to the English before Orleans. In it I told them to depart; a copy of this letter has been read to me here in Rouen. There are two or three sentences in that copy which were not in my letter. For instance, "Give back to the Maiden" should read, "Give back to the King." Also these words, "Troop for troop" and "Commander-in-chief," which were not in my letters.'

In this Joan of Arc was mistaken, M. Fabre points out in his ***Life of the Maid of Orleans***, the text being the same both in the original and in the copy of the letter.

B.--'When at Chinon, could you see as often as you wished him you call your King?'

J.--'I used to go whenever I wished to see my King. When I arrived at the village of Sainte Catherine de Fierbois, I sent a messenger to Chinon to the King. We arrived about mid-day at Chinon, and lodged at an inn. After dinner I went to see the King at the castle.'

Either here Joan of Arc, or the reporter, which is more likely, makes a slip, as she did not see Charles till two days after her arrival at Chinon.

B.--'Who pointed out the King to you?'

J.--'When I entered the chamber I recognised the King from among all the others, my voices having revealed him to me. I told the King that I wished to go and make war on the English.'

B.--'When your voices revealed your King to you, were they accompanied by any light?'

Joan made no answer.

B.--'Did you see any angel above the figure of the King?'

'Spare me such questions,' pleaded Joan; but the Inquisitor was not to be so easily put off, and repeated the question again and again, until Joan said that the King had also seen visions and heard revelations.

'What were these revelations?' asked the priest.

This Joan refused to answer, and told Beaupere that he might, if he liked, send to Charles and ask him.

'Did you expect the King to see you?' then asked the priest.

Her answer was that the voice had promised her that the King would soon see her after her arrival.

'And why,' asked Beaupere, 'did he receive you?'

'Those on my side,' said Joan, 'knew well that I was sent by God; they have known and acknowledged that voice.'

'Who?' asked Beaupere.

'The King and others,' answered Joan, 'have heard the voices coming to me. Charles of Bourbon also, and two or three others.'

(The Charles of Bourbon was the Count of Clermont.)

'Did you often hear that voice?' asked the priest.

'Not a day passes that I do not hear it,' Joan replied.

'What do you ask of it?' inquired Beaupere.

'I have never,' answered Joan, 'asked for any recompense, except the salvation of my soul.'

'Did the voice always encourage you to follow the army?'

'The voice told me to remain at Saint Denis. I wished to remain, but against my will the knights obliged me to leave. I would have remained had I had my free-will.'

'When were you wounded?' asked Beaupere.

'I was wounded,' Joan answered, 'in the moat before Paris, having gone there from Saint Denis. At the end of five days I recovered.'

'What did you attempt to do against Paris?'

Joan answered that she had made one skirmish (escarmouche) in front of Paris.

'Was it on a feast day?' asked the priest.

'It was,' replied Joan. And on being asked if she considered it right to make an attack on such a day, she refused to answer.

It is plain that the gist of those questions made by Beaupere was to try and make Joan of Arc avow that her voices had given her evil counsel. On the following day the same tactics were pursued.

The third meeting of the tribunal was held on the 24th of February, in the same chamber. Sixty-two assessors were present. Again Cauchon commenced by admonishing Joan to tell the truth on all subjects asked her, and again she protested that as far as her revelations were concerned she could give no answers. On Cauchon insisting, she said, 'Take care what you, who are my judge, undertake, for you take a terrible responsibility on yourself, and you presume too far. It is enough,' she added, 'that I have already twice taken the oath.'

Upon her saying this, Cauchon lost all control, and he stormed and threatened her with instant condemnation if she refused to take the oath.

'All the clergy in Paris and Rouen could not condemn me,' was the proud answer, 'if they had not the right to do so.' But, as on the previous occasions, she said she would willingly answer all questions relating to her deeds since leaving her home, but that it would take many days for her to tell them all. Wearied with the persistence and threats of her arch-tormentor, Cauchon, Joan said that she had been sent by God and wished to return to God. 'I have nothing more to do here,' she added.

Beaupere was again ordered to cross-examine the prisoner.

He began by asking her when she had last eaten.

'Not since yesterday at mid-day,' she said. (It was then Lent.)

Beaupere then began again to question her regarding the voice. When had she last heard it?

'On the previous day,' Joan said, 'and also on that day too.'

'At what o'clock of the day before?'

Thrice she had heard the voice in the morning, and once at the hour of Vespers, and again when the ***Ave Maria*** was being sung.

'What were you doing,' asked Beaupere, 'when the voices called you?'

'I was sleeping,' answered Joan, 'and the voice awoke me.'

'Did it awake you by touching your arm?'

'The voice awoke me without its touching me.'

'Was it in your room?'

'Not that I know, but it was in the castle.'

'Did you acknowledge it by kneeling?'

'I acknowledged its presence by sitting up and clasping my hands. I had begged for its help.'

'And what did it say to you?'

'It told me to answer boldly.'

'Tell us more clearly what it said to you.'

'I asked its advice in what I should answer, and bade it ask the Saviour for counsel. And the voice said, "Answer boldly; God will help you."'

'Had it said anything to you before you interrupted it?'

'Some words it had said which I did not clearly comprehend; but when fully awake I understood it to tell me to answer boldly.' Then, emboldened as it seemed by the recollection of that voice, she turned to Cauchon and exclaimed, 'You, Bishop, you tell me that you are my judge--have a care how you act, for in truth I am sent by God, and your position is one of great peril.'

Then Beaupere broke in again, and asked Joan of Arc if the voice had ever altered its advice, and whether it had told Joan not to answer all the questions that would be put to her.

'I cannot answer you about that,' said Joan. 'I have revelations of matters concerning the King which I shall not reveal.'

The Maid then asked whether she might wait for fifteen days, in order that, by that time, she might know whether she might, or might not, answer questions relating to this point.

The priest then asked whether she knew that the voice came from God.

'Yes,' she answered, 'and by this order--that,' she continued, 'I believe as firmly as I believe the Christian religion, and that God has saved us from the pains of hell.'

She was then asked if the voice was that of a male or of a female.

'It is a voice sent by God,' she only deigned to say to this.

Joan again asked for an interval of fifteen days, in order that she might better be able in that time to know how much she might reveal to her judges relating to her voices.

On being asked whether she believed the Almighty would be displeased at her telling the whole truth, she said that she had been ordered by the voices to reveal certain things to the King, and not to her judges; that her voices had told her that very night many things for the good of the King which he alone was to know.

But, asked Beaupere, could she not prevail on the voices to visit the King?

'I know not if the voices would consent,' she answered.

'But why,' then asked Beaupere, 'does the voice not speak to the King now, as it did formerly, when you were with him?'

'I know not if it be the wish of God,' Joan answered: 'without the grace of God I should be able to do nothing.'

This remark, most innocent to our comprehension, was afterwards made use of as a weapon to accuse the prisoner of the charge of heresy.

Later on in the day Beaupere asked Joan if the voice had form and features. This the prisoner refused to answer.

'There is a saying among children,' she said, 'that one is sometimes hanged for speaking the truth.'

On being asked by Beaupere if she was sure of being in a state of grace--a question to which he had carefully led up, and whereby Cauchon hoped to entrap her into a statement which might be used in the accusation of heresy he was now framing against Joan of Arc--her answer even disarmed the Bishop.

'If I am not, may God place me in it; if I am already, may He keep me in it.'

When that test question had been put to the prisoner, one of the judges, guessing the object of its being made, expostulated, to Cauchon's rage--who roughly bade him hold his peace.

To that triumphant reply Joan of Arc added these words: 'If I am not in God's grace I should be the most unhappy being in the world, and I do not think, were I living in sin, that my voices would come to me. Would,' she cried, 'that every one could hear them as well as I do myself!'

Beaupere then asked her about her childhood, and when she had first heard the voices. Asked if there were many people at Domremy in favour of the Burgundians, she said she only knew of one individual. Then came a string of questions about the fairy-well, the haunted oak-tree. All these questions Joan fully answered. She had never, she said, seen a fairy, nor had she heard the prophecy about the oak wood from which a maid was to come and deliver France. When asked if she would leave off wearing man's clothes, she said she would not, as it was the will of Heaven for her to wear them.

The fourth day of the trial was the 27th of February. Fifty-three judges were present. The usual attempt to make Joan take the oath was made to the prisoner by Cauchon, and she was again cross-examined by Beaupere. Again questioned as to her voices, she said that without their permission she could not say what they said to her relating to the King.

Asked if the voices came to her direct from God, or through some intermediary channel, she answered, 'The voices are those of Saint Catherine and Saint Margaret;

they wear beautiful crowns--of this I may speak, for they allow me to do so.' If, she added, her words were doubted, they might send to Poitiers, where she had already been questioned on the same subject.

'How do you distinguish one from the other?' asked Beaupere.

'By the manner in which they salute me,' Joan answered.

'How long have they been in communication with you?'

'I have been under their protection seven years,' was the answer.

Joan had referred to the succour which she had received from Saint Michel. On being asked which of these saints was the first to appear to her, she said it was the last named. She had seen him, she said, as clearly as she saw Beaupere, and that he was not by himself, but in a company of angels. When he left her she felt miserable, and longed to have been taken with the flight of angels.

When Beaupere asked her if it was her own idea to come into France, Joan replied in the affirmative, and also that she would sooner have been torn to pieces by horses than have come without the will of God.

'Does He,' asked the priest, 'tell you not to wear the man's dress? and had not Baudricourt,' he added, 'wished she should dress as a man?'

She said it was not by man's but by God's orders that she wore the dress of a man.

The questions again turned upon the vision and the voice.

Had an angel appeared above the head of the King at Chinon?

She answered that when she entered the King's presence, three hundred soldiers stood in the hall, and fifty torches burnt in the great hall of the castle, and that without counting the spiritual light within.

She was then asked respecting her examination before the clergy at Poitiers.

'They believed,' Joan answered, 'that there was nothing in me against matters of religion.'

Then Beaupere asked the prisoner if she had visited Sainte Catherine de Fierbois.

'Yes,' she answered; 'I heard mass there twice in one day, on my way to Chinon.'

'How did you communicate your message to the King?'

'I sent a letter asking him if I might be allowed to see him. That I had come one hundred and fifty miles to bring him assistance, and that I had much to do for him. I think,' she added, 'that I also said I should know him amongst all those who might be present.'

'Did you then wear a sword?' asked Beaupere.

'I had one that I had taken at Vaucouleurs.'

'Had you not another one as well?'

'Yes; I had sent to the church of Fierbois, either from Troyes or Chinon, for a sword from the back of the altar of Sainte Catherine. It was found, much rusted.'

'How did you know there was a sword there?'

'Through my voices. I asked in a letter that the sword should be given me, and the clergy sent me it. It lay underground--I am not certain whether at the front or at the back of the altar. It was cleaned by the people belonging to the church. They had a scabbard made for me; also one was made at Tours--one of velvet, the other of black cloth. I had also a third one for the Fierbois sword made of very strong leather.'

'Were you wearing that sword,' asked Beaupere, 'when you were captured?'

'No, I had not one then; I used to wear it constantly up to the time that I left Saint Denis, after the assault on Paris.'

'What benediction did you bestow on that sword?'

'None,' said Joan; and she added, on being questioned as to her feeling about the sword, that she had a particular liking for it, from its having been found in the Church of Sainte Catherine, her favourite saint.

Then Beaupere inquired whether Joan was not in the habit of placing this sword on the altar, in order to bring it good luck.

Joan answered in the negative.

'But then,' the priest asked, 'had she not prayed that it might bring her good fortune?'

'It is enough to know,' answered Joan, 'that I wished my armour might bring me good fortune.'

'What had become of the Fierbois sword?' asked the priest.

'I offered up at Saint Denis,' answered Joan, 'a sword and some armour, but not the Fierbois sword.'

'Had you it when at Lagny?' asked Beaupere.

'Yes,' answered the prisoner.

But between the time passed at Lagny and Compiegne she wore another sword, taken from a Burgundian soldier, which she said was a good weapon, able to deal shrewd blows. But she would not satisfy Beaupere's curiosity as to what had become of the sword of Fierbois: 'That,' she said, 'has nothing to do with the trial.'

Beaupere next inquired as to what had become of Joan of Arc's goods.

She said her brother had her horses and her goods; she said she believed the latter amounted to some twelve thousand *ecus*.

'Had you not,' asked the priest, 'when you went to Orleans, a banner or pennon? Of what colour was that?'

'My banner had a field all covered with ***fleurs-de-lis***. In it was represented the world, with angels on either side. It was white, made of white cloth, of a kind called ***coucassin***. On it was written ***Jesu Maria***. It was bordered with silk.'

'Which were you fondest of?' asked Beaupere,--'your banner or your sword?'

'I loved my banner,' was the answer, 'forty times as much as I did my sword.'

'Who painted your banner?'

This Joan would not say.

'Who bore your flag?' asked the priest.

Joan of Arc said she carried it herself when charging the enemy, 'in order,' she added, 'to avoid killing any one. I never killed any one,' she said.

'How many soldiers did the King give you,' asked the priest, 'when he gave you a command?'

'Between ten and twelve thousand men,' answered Joan.

Then Beaupere questioned her regarding the relief of Orleans, and he was told by the Maid that she first went to the redoubt of Saint Loup by the bridge.

'Did you expect,' was the next question, 'that you would be able to raise the siege?'

'Yes,' she was certain, Joan answered, from a revelation which she had received, and of which she had told the King before making the expedition.

'At the time of the assault,' asked Beaupere, 'did you not tell your soldiers that you alone would receive all the arrows, bolts, and stones discharged by the cannon and culverins?'

'No,' she answered, 'there were over a hundred wounded; but,' she added, 'I said to my people, "Be assured that you will raise the siege."'

'Were you wounded?' asked the priest.

'I was wounded,' Joan answered, 'at the assault of the fortress on the bridge. I was struck and wounded by an arrow or a dart; but I received much comfort from Saint Catherine, and I recovered in less than fifteen days. I recovered, and in spite of the wound I did not give up riding or working.'

'Did you know beforehand that you would be wounded?' asked Beaupere.

'Yes,' was the answer; 'and I had told my King I should be wounded. My saints had told me of it.'

'In what manner were you wounded?' he asked.

'I was,' she answered, 'the first to raise a ladder against the fortress at the bridge. While raising the ladder I was struck by the bolt.'

'Why,' now asked the priest, 'did you not come to terms with the English captains at Jargeau?'

'The knights about me,' she answered, 'told the English that they could not have a truce of fifteen days, which they wanted; but that they and their horses must leave the place at once.'

'And what did you say?'

'I told them that if they left the place with their side arms (petites cottes) their lives would be spared. If not, that Jargeau would be stormed.'

'Had you then consulted your voices to know whether you should accord them that delay or not?'

Joan did not remember.

Here closed the fourth day's trial.

The fifth day of the trial took place on the 1st of March. Fifty-eight judges were present.

The opening proceedings were the same as on the former occasions, and Joan of Arc again professed her willingness to answer all questions put to her regarding her deeds as readily as if she were in the presence of the Pope of Rome himself; but, as formerly, she gave no promise of revealing what her voices had told her.

Beaupere caught immediately at the opportunity of her having spoken of the Pope to lay a pitfall in her path: Which Pope did she believe the authentic one--he at Avignon or the one in Rome?

'Are there two?' she asked. This was an awkward question to those bishops and doctors of the faith who had for so long a time encouraged the schism in the Church.

Beaupere evaded the question, and asked her if it were true that she had received a letter from the Count of Armagnac asking her which of the two Popes he was bound to obey.

A copy of this letter was produced, as well as the one sent by Joan of Arc in reply.

When she sent her answer, the Maid said, she was about to mount her horse, and had told him she would be able better to answer his question when at rest in Paris or elsewhere. The copy of her letter which was now read, Joan said, did not quite agree with that she had sent to Armagnac.

'She had not,' Joan added, 'said in her letter that what she knew was by the inspiration of Heaven.'

Again pressed as to which of the two Popes she believed the true one, she said that the one then in Rome was to her that one.

Questioned regarding her letter to the English before Orleans, she acknowledged the accurateness of the copy produced, with the exception of a slight mistake. She retracted nothing regarding this letter, and declared that the English would, ere seven years were passed from that time, give a more striking proof of their loss of power in France than that which they had shown before Orleans. This prediction was literally carried out when, in 1436, Paris opened its gates to Charles VII., the loss of the capital being shortly after followed by the loss of all the other English conquests, with the exception of the town of Calais--the gains of a century of war being snatched from them in a score of years.

'They will meet,' said Joan of Arc, 'with greater reverses than have yet befallen them.'

When she was asked what made her speak thus, she answered that these things had been revealed to her. The examination again turned upon her voices and apparitions.

'Do they always appear to you in the same dress? Always in the same form, and richly crowned?'

Similar foolish questions were then put to her. Had the saints long hair? She did not know. And what language did they converse in with her?

'Their language,' she replied, 'is good and beautiful.'

'What sort of voices were theirs?'

'They speak to me in soft and beautiful French voices,' she said.

'Does not Saint Margaret speak in English?'

'How should she,' was the answer, 'when she is not on the side of the English?'

'Do they wear ear-rings?'

This Joan could not say; but the idiotic question reminded the prisoner that Cauchon had taken a ring from her. She had worn two--one had been taken by the Burgundians when she was captured, the other by the Bishop. The former had been given her by her parents, the latter by one of her brothers. This ring she asked Cauchon to give the Church.

'Had she not,' she was asked, 'made use of these rings to heal the sick?'

She had never done so.

It is very easy throughout all these questionings to see how eager Cauchon and the other judges were to find some acknowledgment from the lips of Joan of Arc, upon which they could found a charge of heresy against her. Her visions were distorted by them into a proof of infernal agency; even the harmless superstitions of her village home did not escape being turned into idolatrous and infernal matters of belief.

Had not her saints, questioned the Bishop, appeared to her beneath the haunted oak of Domremy?--and what had they promised her besides the re-establishment of Charles upon the throne?

'They promised,' she answered, 'to take me with them to Paradise, which I had prayed them to do.'

'Nothing more?' queried Cauchon.

'If they made me another promise,' Joan replied, 'I am not at liberty to say what that promise is till three months are past.'

'Did they say that you would be free in three months' time?'

That question remained unanswered, but before those three months had passed, the heroine had been delivered by death from all earthly sufferings.

She was again minutely questioned regarding the superstitions of her country.

Was there not growing there a certain fabulous plant, called Mandragora? Joan of Arc knew nothing regarding such a plant--had never seen it, and did not know the use of it. Again the apparitions were brought forward.

'What was Saint Michel like? Was he clothed?'

'Do you think,' was the answer to this question, which could only have occurred to a foul-minded priest, 'do you think that God cannot clothe him?'

Other absurd questions followed--as to his hair; long or short? Had he a pair of scales with him? As before, Joan of Arc answered these futile, and sometimes indecent, questions with her wonderful patience. At one moment she could not help exclaiming how supremely happy the sight of her saints made her; it seemed as if a sudden vision of her beloved saints had been vouchsafed her in the midst of that crowd of persecuting priests.

She was again told to tell what the sign or secret was which she had revealed to the King on first seeing him at Chinon; but about this she was firm as adamant, and refused to give any information. To reveal that sign or secret would, she felt, be not only a breach of confidence and disloyalty between her and her King, but a crime to divulge a sacred secret, which Charles kept sealed in his breast, and which she was determined to utter to no one, and least of all to his enemies.

'I have already said,' she told her judges, 'that you will have nothing from me about that. Go and ask the King!'

Then followed questions as to the fashion of the crown that the King had worn at Rheims: which brought the fifth day of the trial to a close.

The sixth and last day's public examination took place on the 3rd of March, forty-two judges present. The long series of questions were nearly all relating to the appearance of the saints. Both questions and answers were nearly the same as on the previous occasions, and little more information was got from the prisoner.

After these, the subject of her dress--what she then wore, and what she had worn--was entered upon.

'When you came to the King,' she was asked, 'did he not inquire if your change in dress was owing to a revelation or not?'

'I have already answered,' said Joan, 'that I do not remember if he asked me. This evidence was made known when I was at Poitiers.'

'And the doctors who examined you,' asked Beaupere, 'at Poitiers, did they not want to know regarding your being dressed in man's clothes?'

'I don't remember,' she answered; 'but they asked me when I had first begun to wear man's dress, and I told them that it was when I was at Vaucouleurs.'

She was then asked whether the Queen had not asked her to leave off wearing male clothes. She answered that that had nothing to do with the trial.

'But,' next inquired Beaupere, 'when you were at the castle of Beaurevoir, did not the ladies there ask you to do so?'

'Yes,' was the answer, 'and they offered to give me a woman's dress. But the time had not yet come.' She would, she added, have yielded sooner to the wishes of those ladies than to those of any other, the Queen excepted.

The subject of the flags and banners used by her during her campaigns was now entered on.

Had her standards not been copied by the men-at-arms?

'They did so at their pleasures,' she answered.

'Of what material was the banner made? If the poles were broken, were they renewed?'

'They were,' she answered, 'when broken.'

'Did you not,' asked Beaupere, 'say that the flags made like your banners were of good augury?'

'What I said,' answered Joan, 'to my soldiers was, that they should attack the enemy with boldness.'

'Did you not sprinkle holy water on the banners?'

To this question Joan refused to answer.

Next she was questioned about a certain Friar Richard, the preaching friar who had seen her at Troyes. She answered that he came to her making the sign of the Cross, and that she told him to come up to her without fear.

She was asked if it was true that she had pictures painted of herself in the likeness of a saint.

'When at Arras,' she answered, 'she had seen a portrait of herself, in which she was represented kneeling before the King and presenting him with a letter.'

'But was there not a picture of you,' asked Beaupere, 'in your host's house at Orleans?'

Joan of Arc knew nothing regarding such a picture.

'Did you not know,' was the next question put, 'that your partisans had prayers and masses said in your honour?'

'If they did so,' she answered, 'it was not by my wish; but if they prayed for me,' she added, 'there was no harm in so doing.'

She was then asked what her opinion was regarding the people who kissed her hands and her feet, and even her clothes. She answered that, inasmuch as she could, she prevented them doing so; but she acknowledged that the poor people flocked eagerly around her, and that she gave them all the assistance in her power.

She was next asked if she had not stood sponsor to some children baptized at Rheims.

'Not at Rheims,' she said; but she had for one child at Troyes. She had also stood sponsor for two children at Saint Denis, and she had gladly had the boy christened by the name of Charles in honour of the King, and the girl Joan, as it pleased their mothers.

'Did the women not touch your rings and charms?'

'Many,' she answered, 'were wont to touch both my hands and my rings; but I know not with what intention.'

'Did she not receive the sacrament and confess herself as she passed through the country?'

'Often,' she answered.

'And did you,' asked the priest, 'receive the sacrament in your male attire?'

'Yes,' she said; 'but not, if I recollect right, when wearing my armour.'

This confession of having received the Eucharist in her male dress was made one of the accusations of sacrilege by Joan of Arc's judges.

She was next questioned about a horse she had bought from the Bishop of Senlis, and ridden in battle.

The next point related to the supposed miraculous resurrection--a very temporary one however--of an infant three days old at Lagny. When Joan was in that place, this child appeared to have died, and was put before the image of the Virgin, in front of which some young women were kneeling. Joan of Arc joined them in their prayers, upon which it was noticed that the supposed dead infant gave some signs of life; he or she was baptized, and soon after expired. Joan of Arc had never for a moment supposed that it was owing to her presence and her prayers that this miracle had occurred.

'But,' asked Beaupere, 'was it not the common talk of the town of Lagny that you had performed this miracle, and had been the means of restoring the infant to life?'

'I did not inquire,' she said.

She was then asked about the woman, Catherine de la Rochelle, whom, it may be remembered, Joan had discovered to be a vulgar impostor, and whom she had tried to dissuade from making people believe that she could discover hidden treasures, advising her to return to her husband and her children.

Next she was asked why she had tried to escape from her prison tower at Beaurevoir. She said that she had made the attempt, although against the warning of her voices, which had counselled her to have patience--but that Saint Catherine had comforted her after her fall from the tower, telling her that she would recover, and also that Compiegne would not be taken.

It was tried to prove that in order not to fall into the hands of the enemy she intended committing suicide. To this accusation she answered:--

'I have already said that I would sooner give up my soul into God's keeping, than fall into the hands of the English.'

And with this ended the sixth and last public day of the heroine's trial.

Joan of Arc's judges had found nothing to attach guilt to her in any of her replies; but as she had been condemned before the farce was enacted of trying her, her innocence could not save her life. As Michelet observes, Joan of Arc's answers may have had some effect in touching the hearts of even such men as were her judges; and it was perhaps on this account that Cauchon thought it more prudent to continue holding the trial with only a few, and those few picked men, of whose sympathies, characters, and feelings he was sure. The Bishop's ostensible reason in having the trial henceforth carried on in private was in order 'not to tire the others.' A most thoughtful and tender-hearted Bishop! The details of the trial were now placed in the hands of two judges and two witnesses. Cauchon now felt he had a free hand. On the 12th of March he had obtained the permission of the Grand Inquisitor of the Holy Office in France to make use of the services of his Vicar-General--his name, as has already been said, was John Lemaitre.

The first of the long series of secret interrogations was held in Joan of Arc's prison--probably in the principal tower--on the 10th of March.

John de la Fontaine questioned the prisoner as follows:--

'When you went to Compiegne from which place did you start?'

'From Crespy-en-Valois.'

'When you arrived at Compiegne did many days elapse before you made the sortie?'

'I arrived secretly at an early hour of the morning, and entered the town so that the enemy could not be aware of my arrival, and the same day, in the evening, I made the sortie in which I was captured.'

'Were the bells of the church rung on the occasion of your arrival?'

'If they were, it was not by my command. I had not given it a thought.'

'Did you not order them to be rung?'

'I have no recollection of having done so.'

'Did you make the sortie by the command of your voices?'

'Last Easter, when in the trenches of Melun, the voices of Saint Catherine and Saint Margaret told me I should be taken prisoner before St. John's Day; but that I was to keep a brave heart, and take all that befell me with patience, and that in the end God would come to my aid.'

'Since then, did your voices tell you that you would be taken?'

'Yes, often; nearly every day; and I implored my voices that when I was taken I might then die, and not suffer a long imprisonment: and the voices said, "Be without fear, for these things must happen." But they did not tell me the time when I should be taken, for had I known that I should not have made that sortie.'

'Did you not question them about the time in which you would be taken?'

'I often inquired; but they never told me.'

'Did your voices cause you to make that sortie, and not tell you the manner by which you would be captured?'

'Had I known the hour of my capture I should not have gone out voluntarily; but had my voices ordered me to go and I had known, then would I have gone all the same, whatever might have happened.'

'When you made the sally did you pass over the bridge at Compiegne?'

'I passed over the bridge and along the redoubt; and I charged with my soldiers against John de Luxembourg's men. Twice were they driven back as far as the quarters of the Burgundians; the third time half as far. While so engaged the English arrived, and cut off our communications. While returning towards the bridge, I was taken in the meadows on the side nearest to Picardy.'

'Upon your banner, the one you carried, was not a picture painted representing the world and two angels? What was the significance of that?'

'My saints told me to carry that banner boldly.'

'Did you not also bear arms and a shield?'

'Not I; but the King gave my brothers a coat-of-arms; a shield with a blue ground, on which were two *fleurs-de-lis* of gold, and a sword between.'

'Did you make a present to your brothers of those arms?'

'They were given my brothers by the King, without any request made by me.'

'What kind of horse were you riding when you were captured?'

'I was mounted on a *demi-coursier*.'

'Who had given you that horse?'

'My King,' answered Joan of Arc; and she went on to tell them how she had had fine horses purchased by the King for her use; she also gave them an account of her few possessions.

There is, indeed, so much repetition in the questions and answers during these long examinations, that it would be a weariness to the reader did one minutely rewrite them as they appear in the chronicle. We shall therefore confine ourselves to the principal and most important facts and statements which bear most prominently on our heroine's career, and on the answers most characteristic made by her.

The remainder of that first day's trial in the prison consisted nearly entirely of trying to elicit from Joan of Arc what was the special sign or secret that she had revealed to the King at Chinon. She, however, gave them no further information than in saying that the sign was a beautiful and honoured mark of Divine favour. For hours she was urged to tell of what this special sign or token consisted--whether of precious stones, gold, or silver. Joan, who apparently was wearied out by the pertinacity of her inquisitors, seems to have allowed herself to mix with the reality the fabulous, and described that an angel had appeared to Charles bringing him a crown of matchless beauty. She seems, poor creature, half dazed and bewildered by her sufferings and her tormentors, to have mixed up in her mind and in her replies the actual event of the King's coronation at Rheims with her angelic visions and voices;

for to her one must have appeared as real and actual as the other.

Nine examinations in the prison tower of Rouen were undergone by Joan of Arc:--Once on the 10th of March; twice on the 12th, and again on the 13th; twice on the 14th; again on the 15th; and twice more on the 17th. In all these successive trials, nothing of importance was obtained by the judges from the prisoner. Both answers and questions were similar to those which have already been recorded during the days of her examinations in public. Throughout all this trying process of a week's long and minute cross-questioning, the heroine maintained the same firmness, and answered with the same simple dignity as on the former occasions. Two of her answers may be justly called sublime. When during the course of the seventh day's trial, she was asked what doctrine Saint Michel had inspired her with, she answered:--

'The pity that I have for the Kingdom of France!'

And again, when at the close of the last day's examination she was asked why she had taken such special care that her banner should be carried and held near the King during the ceremony of the coronation, she answered:--

'If it had been in the travail it was right that it should be in the place of greatest honour.' ('Il avait ete a la peine; c'etait bien raison qu'il fut a l'honneur!')

Glorious words, worthy of her who spoke them! They bear with them an heroic ring, and reveal by one sublime expression the very soul and spirit of Joan of Arc!

Little as the secret interrogations had revealed to Joan of Arc's examiners regarding the mysterious sign they were so eager to wrest from her, Cauchon had succeeded in inveigling his victim into making statements he considered could be used in a charge of heresy against her.

When bidden to say if she would be ready to submit herself regarding all her actions to the determination of the Church, she answered that she loved the Church, and was ready to obey its doctrines as far as lay in her power; and on being asked to which Church she alluded, whether to the Church Militant or to the Church Triumphant, she replied, 'I have been sent to France by God and the Virgin Mary, and by the saints of the Church Victorious from above, and to that Church I submit myself, and all that I have done or may have to do!'

This answer did not satisfy Cauchon, and he again inquired to which Church she submitted; but Joan had already answered, and would say no more--and on this Cauchon fixed his accusation of heresy against the heroine. Having failed throughout the trial to get Joan to say anything incriminating regarding Charles VII. or anything which might tend to injure him in the minds of his subjects, Cauchon had Joan questioned as to what she thought respecting the murder of the Duke of Orleans by Charles.

'It was a great misfortune for the kingdom of France,' was her answer.

Could the wariest statesman have better parried that question? Not on one single occasion during the long series of questions that Joan of Arc was made to undergo, without any counsel or help, and with some of the subtlest brains in the country eager to involve her in damaging statements and to entangle her in saying something which might be taken up as injurious to Charles--that mean prince, who made so much by her devotion to him and his cause, and in return for that devotion had not taken a step towards attempting her deliverance--not at any time did she drop one word or let an expression escape her which could cause any uneasiness to the King, who had proved himself so utterly unworthy of such a subject, or to the men about the King's person, some of whom, if not actually guilty of having given her over to her enemies, at any rate had allowed her to be kept during all those long months a close prisoner, without protest or any sign of sympathy.

When the judges asked Joan if she were as willing to answer the questions put to her, standing in the presence of the Pope, as she had done in the presence of the Bishop of Beauvais, she replied that she would willingly do so. The idea of referring her case to the Pope was not at all what Cauchon wished to enter her mind; and when he found that John de la Fontaine and two monks had visited the prisoner and advised her to submit herself to Rome, he was furious, and threatened them with condign punishment. They only escaped the Bishop's anger by taking flight from Rouen. It was not too soon for Cauchon's object that the trial was now conducted with closed doors. Joan of Arc's courage, firmness, and simplicity, accompanied by her transparent truth and pure fervent belief in her mission, impressed even her judges--and much more so those who had attended the public days of her trial as spectators. Now and again, after one of her straightforward and brave answers, which would expose and lay bare the malicious intention of the question, voices were heard to say in the great hall, 'Well spoken, Joan!' and an English knight was overheard to declare that, for his part, he regretted that such a courageous maid had not been born an Englishwoman. A reaction in favour of the heroine might have set in, and, as we have already said, it was for fear of this that Cauchon caused the trial in future to be held in private. It is clear from the previous narrative that the prisoner had no one to advise her, no one to support her. At the commencement of the trial she asked to be allowed counsel, but Cauchon refused this most just demand. Among the crowd of doctors and clergy it was impossible but that, now and again, some feeling of interest, even of sympathy, should gain a few of these men, who, in spite of their education and surroundings, were human beings after all. But whenever such feeling was shown, Cauchon, ever on the watch, sternly repressed its manifestation. The name of Isambard de la Pierre should be remembered for good; for he, although one of the creatures of the detestable Inquisition, showed humanity to Cauchon's victim. During the examinations it was the wont of Isambard to place himself as near as possible to Joan of Arc, and by nudging her, or by some sign, he attempted to help her and advise her in her answers to the questions of the judges. Cauchon's evil eye, however, at length detected Isambard's conduct, and he informed Warwick of it. Soon after, Isambard was confronted by Warwick, and the latter, with many abusive words, threatened to have him drowned in the Seine if he dared assist Joan of Arc.

Though the Maid's treatment in the dungeon of the castle was not, after the beginning of the trial, so barbarous as in the first days after her arrival at Rouen, when she was treated like a caged wild animal, the poor prisoner was watched day and night by three soldiers, who, one must fear, outraged every sense of humanity in their treatment of Joan. The very term ***houspiller*** proves that they were set apart to embitter the prisoner's already too cruel state. Although Joan of Arc never herself disclosed the abominable fact, the reason for retaining and continuing to wear her male dress was that it served her as a protection from these ruffians. Chained to a heavy wooden beam, her sufferings must have been at times almost beyond endurance; but in this long torture, which was only to terminate in the flaming death, her wonderful constancy and heaven-inspired spirit never failed. Had she given way to a kind of despair, as happened shortly before her final release--for only a few moments indeed--her jailers would not have neglected to record such weakness as a sign that her heavenly agencies had failed, if not forsaken her utterly. What appears to have constituted the greatest privation to Joan of Arc during her imprisonment was not being allowed the consolation of receiving the rites of the religion she so fervently believed. During the days on which the public examinations were held in the hall of the castle, she was wont to be led from her dungeon by a passage leading to the place of judgment: the castle chapel was passed in traversing this passage. One day while going by the chapel door she asked one of the sheriffs, Massieu, whether the Eucharist was then exposed within the chapel, and, if so, whether she might be permitted to kneel before the entrance. The man was humane enough to allow her to do so, but this coming to the knowledge of one of Cauchon's familiars, the sheriff was told if he allowed the prisoner again to kneel before the chapel door that he would be thrown into prison--'and,' added Cauchon, 'in a prison where no light of sun or moon should appear!'

But perhaps among so many instances of cruelty and bigotry, the most infamous act of all the many in this tragedy was that performed by the Canon Nicolas Loiseleur, a creature of Cauchon, as false, as cruel, and as unscrupulous as his master and patron. This reverend scoundrel had, at the beginning of the trial, by his feigned sympathy for the prisoner, wormed himself into Joan of Arc's confidence. He told her that he, too, came from near her home, that he in his heart of hearts belonged to the French side, that he was a prisoner on account of his known devotion to Charles and to France, and many other such lies. This Judas--half in the character of a layman, half in that of a confessor, and wholly as a sympathetic friend and a fellow-sufferer--paid the prisoner long visits, disguised both as priest and layman, as the part suited the day's action best. Loiseleur actually used the means of extracting information from Joan of Arc under the seal of confession, to be afterwards employed against her by Cauchon. While these conversations and confessions took place, Warwick and Cauchon would be concealed in a part of the dungeon from which they could overhear what passed between the two--one of whom worthily might be called an angel, the other truthfully a devil. With the Bishop and knight--whose conduct as regards Joan of Arc deeply tarnished an otherwise high character--were seated clerks, who wrote down what passed in these meetings. The clerks, to their credit, are said to have at first refused to comply with doing such dirty work.

Cauchon gained but little by this infamy. Nothing of any importance could be constructed out of the prisoner's confidence and confessions; but Cauchon was, through Loiseleur, enabled to tender such advice to Joan as made her answers coincide more closely with his wishes than they otherwise could have done; especially those relating to the Church Triumphant and Militant.

When his crime had borne fruit, Loiseleur, like another Judas, was overwhelmed with an intolerable remorse; and, although he obtained his victim's pardon, his end appears to have been as sudden as that of Judas, if not also self-inflicted. By a lawyer named John Lohier, whom he consulted during the course of the trial, Cauchon was not so well served as he had been by Loiseleur. This Lohier, who was a Norman and seems to have been a worthy man, had the courage to tell Cauchon that inasmuch as Joan of Arc was being tried in secret and without benefit of counsel, the proceedings were null and worthless. Like all who showed any interest for the prisoner, Lohier was threatened by Cauchon with imprisonment, but he escaped and found refuge in Rome.

On Passion Sunday, the 18th of March, Cauchon held a meeting of a dozen of the lawyers, including the Vice-Inquisitor, and asked them to give their opinion on some of the answers of Joan of Arc. He held a second and similar consistory on the 22nd of that month, at which it was decided to shape into the form of a series of articles the chief heads of accusation. This, when made out, was to be submitted to the prisoner. On the 24th, the Bishop, accompanied by the Vice-Inquisitor and some others, proceeded to the dungeon in which Joan of Arc was kept. The day was Palm Sunday, and the great French historian Michelet has, with his accustomed skill and bright, vivid word-painting, in his short but incomparable *Life* of the heroine not only of France but of humanity, reminded his readers with what a longing Joan of Arc must, on that festival of joy and triumph, have yearned for the privilege 'to breathe once again the fresh air of heaven.' Daughter of the fields, born on the border of the woods, she who had always lived under the open sky had to pass Easter Day in a dark dungeon tower. To her the great succour which the Church invokes upon that day did not reach--her prison door did not fly open.

It may be recalled that on Palm Sunday the morning prayer in the office of the Roman Church contains these words: 'Deus in adjutorium meum intende.' For her, however, no earthly gate was to be thrown open wide. The gate through which she was to pass from suffering and death into life eternal and peace everlasting--(per angusta ad augusta)--was, however, not far distant. But she had still to wait awhile amid the ever-darkening shadows.

'If,' said Cauchon to Joan, 'you will cease to wear this man's dress, and dress as you would do were you back in your home, you shall be allowed to hear Mass.'

But Joan could not be prevailed on to consent to abandon the costume, which, as we have said, proved her safeguard against the brutality of her jailers.

By the 26th of March the articles were drawn up and ready, and were approved of in a meeting held by Cauchon in his own house. And on these articles, or rather heads of articles, the further trial of the prisoner was to be carried on.

The examination took place on the days following in a chamber next to the great hall in the castle. Nine judges, besides Cauchon, attended. The Bishop ordered Joan to answer categorically all the accusations on which she was arraigned; if she refused to do so, or remained silent beyond a given time, he threatened her with excommunication. He went on to declare that all her judges were men of high position, well versed in all matters appertaining to Church and State; and he had the audacity to qualify them--and probably included himself among them--as being ***benins et pitoyables***, having no wish to inflict corporal punishment upon Joan, but filled only with the pious desire of leading her into the way of truth and salvation. 'Seeing that,' he continued, 'she was not sufficiently versed in such weighty matters as those they had now to deal with, they in their pitifulness and benignity, would allow her to choose among the learned doctors present, one or more to aid her with counsel and advice.'

The Bishop had probably guessed that by this time Joan of Arc would have ceased to care for the benefit of counsel, having had to do without it till now; and his asking her whether she wished for it was merely made in order to appear as an act of judicial indulgence on his part--perhaps, also, what Lohier had urged regarding the illegality of trying his prisoner without giving her the help of counsel may have influenced him.

In a few simple words Joan of Arc thanked the Bishop and the others for the offer, of which she, however, declined to avail herself. She added that she felt no need now of having any human counsel, for that she had that of her Lord to aid her.

Thomas de Courcelles next proceeded to read the articles contained in the act of accusation. These were so long that they occupied the remainder of that and the next day's sitting. This first series of articles--for there were forty more to follow--

-consisted of thirty heads, and forms one of the most glaring examples of what the human mind is capable of inventing when thoroughly steeped in bigotry, stupidity, and cruelty. The Bishop of Beauvais may have been congratulated on producing the most momentous mass of accusation, intended to destroy the life and reputation of a peerless and perfect woman and to blast the career of his native sovereign: it only redounded to the Bishop's everlasting shame and infamy.

We will spare the reader a detailed summary of these articles--articles which have the lie so palpably and strongly writ all over them, that we can but hesitate whether to be more surprised or disgusted that even such a man as Cauchon could dare to bring them into court.

The preamble of the articles gave the gist of what was to follow, and showed up the true spirit of Joan's 'benign and merciful judges.' It consisted of one long string of abuse, in which the terms 'sorceress,' 'false prophet,' 'a practiser of magic,' and 'devilish arts,' were freely used. Joan of Arc was declared in this preamble to be 'abominable in the eyes of God and man'; a violator of all laws--divine, ecclesiastical and natural. To sum up all the epithets, she was termed 'heretical, or, at any rate, strongly suspected of being so.' This accusation, the most awful that those cruel times held, must have sounded to all those men present as the heroine's knell of doom.

Then followed the thirty articles of accusation. Never, indeed, had a short but well filled career, bright with glorious deeds, undertaken for King and fatherland--never had such a life (for no life ever approached that of the Maid's) been so ludicrously, so violently and wilfully misrepresented. Her most innocent words and actions were turned into accusations of sorcery, witchcraft, vice, and every kind of wickedness. Her harmless and pure youth was made to appear a childhood of sorcery and idolatrous superstition; she was accused in her earliest years of having trafficked with evil spirits: it was alleged that she had consorted with witches; that she had frequented places where spirits and fairies best loved to congregate; that she had taken part in sacrilegious dancing; that she had suspended wreaths on the trees in honour of these rural spirits; that she had carried hidden about her person a plant called Mandragora, hoping by it to obtain good luck; that she had left her parents against their will to go to Neufchateau, and lived in that place among a debauched set of people: that in consequence of all these wicked acts, a youth who intended marrying her had not done so. Then, having left not a stage or an act of her innocent girlhood unblasted, and covered with the slime of the Bishop's reptile-like imagination, her acts when with the King were reviewed. She had promised Charles to slay all the English in France; her cruelty and love of bloodshed were insatiable; she had influenced Charles by acts of magic; her banners and her rings were bewitched; she was schismatic, and doubted as to which was the right Pope; and, in spite of this, she had the wickedness to inform the Earl of Armagnac which of the two Popes he was to believe the genuine. Of all this long tissue of crimes laid to her charge, that of wearing a man's dress was made the most heinous; for the Almighty had made it a crime abominable to Himself, that woman should wear man's dress. Now, not only had the prisoner committed this sin, but she had added to it by affirming that she did so by the wish of God--she had done even worse; for did she not refuse when at the castle of Beaurevoir to wear woman's dress, also when at Arras, and even now in Rouen? So obstinate was she in her wickedness that she had refused to comply with the Bishop's wish that she should leave off these clothes, although he had told her she would be allowed to assist at the offices of the Church if she would consent to do so.

To all these accusations, at the end of each paragraph, Cauchon bade Courcelles, who read the accusations, to pause, and would then ask the prisoner what answer she had to make to that accusation. Joan of Arc contented herself by simply denying the alleged crime, or else she referred to the answers she had made to the same, or similar questions, during the former days when under examination. Some of her replies were, as they often had been during those trials, grand in their simplicity. For instance, when asked a difficult and even perplexing question relating to her belief in the Church Militant, she said:--'I believe that the Holy Father, the Bishops, and other clergy, are here for the protection of the Christian faith, and to punish those who deserve it. As to my acts,' she continued, 'I submit them to the Church in Heaven, to God, to the Holy Virgin, and the Saints in Paradise. I have not failed,' she proudly added, 'in the Christian religion; nor will I ever do so.'

When repeatedly questioned about the change of costume, and of its importance regarding her being allowed to attend Mass or not, she said: 'In the eyes of the Saviour the dress of those who receive the Sacrament can have no importance.'

On the day after, the 28th of March, the same chamber was used for the trial, and the same indictments were entered on. That almost interminable series of accusations numbered some seventy charges. On that day, Joan of Arc appears to have ceased to deny at any length the string of false evidence brought against her; she generally replied that she had already answered as to the crimes laid to her charge, or simply said, 'I refer myself to my Saviour.' Two of her answers are worth recording: the first, when accused of having been guilty not only of discarding the proper dress of her sex, but also of having acted the part of a man, she said: 'As to women's occupation there are plenty of them to occupy themselves with such things'; and to the second question, when taunted with having carried out her mission with violence and slaughter, she answered: 'I implored at the commencement of my mission that peace might be made, while, at the same time, I declared that if that was not agreed to, I was willing to fight.' When she was accused of having made war on the Burgundians and the English alike, she made the distinguishing difference between them by saying:--'As to the Duke of Burgundy, I wrote to him, and asked him through his envoys that peace should be made between him and my King. As regards the English, the only peace that could be made with them is when they have returned to England.' The Maid's natural modesty and simplicity are apparent in a circumstance which occurred in one of those long days of searching examination and cross-questioning. When the sentence she had used, and which had been noted down in the minutes of an early day of the trial, was read as follows: 'All that I have done has been done by the advice of my Saviour,' she stopped the clerk, and said that it should stand thus: 'All that I have done well has been done by the advice of my Saviour.' When she was asked by what form of words she prayed to her Saints to come to her assistance, she repeated the following prayer:--'Very blessed God, in honour of your holy Passion, I beseech you, if you love me, that you will reveal to me what I am to answer these Churchmen. I know concerning the dress the reason for which I have adopted it, but I know not in what manner I am to discard it. For this thing I beseech you to tell me what to do.' And she added that after this prayer her voices were soon heard.

On the 31st of March, Cauchon, accompanied by the Vice-Inquisitor and some other of the judges, had an interview with the prisoner. They again inquired of Joan of Arc whether she submitted herself wholly and entirely into the hands of the Church Militant. She answered that if such were her Saviour's wish she was quite willing to do so. The accusations were now set forth afresh, in twelve chief heads or articles, under which the series of calumnies was summarised before they should be submitted to the University of Paris. These twelve heads, which formed the foundation of Joan of Arc's condemnation, were never shown her; and she had therefore no chance of contradicting any of the grossly false charges of which they were full. Like the trial itself, these articles were merely a sham invented for the purpose of throwing dust in the eyes of the people, who by these, it was hoped, would be persuaded that the law of the Church and State had been acted up to. The heads of these articles were as follows:--

First--A woman pretends to have had communication with Saints from her thirteenth year; and she affirms that they have counselled her to dress in male attire; she affirms that she has found her salvation, and refuses to submit herself to the Church.

Second--She affirms that, through a sign, she persuaded the King to believe in her; and that accompanied by an angel she placed a crown upon his head.

Third--She affirms her companionship with Saint Michel and other Saints.

Fourth--She affirms certain things will occur by the revelation obtained by her from certain Saints.

Fifth--She affirms that her wearing a man's dress is done by her through the will of God; she has sinned by receiving the Sacrament in that garb, which she says she would sooner die than quit wearing.

Sixth--She admits having written letters signed with the names of Jesus and Mary and with the sign of a cross. That, also, she admits having threatened death to those who would not obey her; and she affirms that all she has done has been accomplished by the Divine will.

Seventh--She gives a false account of her journey to Vaucouleurs and to Chinon.

Eighth--She also gives an untrue account of her attempt to kill herself at Beaurevoir, sooner than fall into the power of the English.

Ninth--And also gives false statements of her assurance of salvation, provided she remains a maid, and of never having committed any sin.

Tenth--And also of her pretending that Saints Catherine and Margaret speak to her in French, and not in English, as they do not belong to the latter side.

Eleventh--She admits the adoration of her Saints; her disobedience to her parents; and of saying that if the evil one were to appear in the likeness of Saint Michel she would know it was not the Saint.

Twelfth--Admits that she refuses to submit to the Church Militant, and this in spite of being told that all faithful members of the Church must, by the article 'Unam Sanctam Ecclesiam Catholicam,' comply with and submit to the commands of the Church Militant, and principally in all things which pertain to sacred doctrines and the ecclesiastical sanctions.

This was the substance of the twelve articles which Cauchon laid before the doctors of theology and law in Paris. No one knew better than the Bishop how false these were; Manchon himself had been so impressed with their utter fraudulence that he had inserted in their margin, under the date of the 4th of April, the statement that in many instances the facts alleged were entirely at variance with the declarations of the prisoner. Cauchon despatched the articles to Paris on the following day, April the 5th. M. Wallon, in his admirable and exhaustive history of Joan of Arc, has remarked that all her deeds were in these twelve articles travestied from acts of piety or patriotism into acts of superstition and rebellion against God and His Church. 'What,' asks M. Wallon, 'had her accusers to reproach her with? Her visions? None of her judges could declare these were impossible, for then they would declare themselves unbelievers in the history of all the saints, which is full of such visions. They might deny them if they pleased, but it required all the wilful blindness of passion to affirm, once such things were articles of belief, that they came from Satanic influence.' As regards Joan of Arc's costume, she had on several occasions answered with sufficient clearness, and every person might have made a like answer, that there is no hard and fast law laid down by the Church relating to the costume that may be worn by members of the Church. Nay more, it was notorious that one of the female saints of the Church (Sainte Marine) had always worn a man's dress. The question as to her dress had been gone into thoroughly during Joan of Arc's examination by the Churchmen and laymen at Poitiers; that which the Church had not blamed at Poitiers could not therefore be a sin in Rouen. By the same token, how was it possible for Joan to believe that what had not been disapproved of by the Archbishop at Rheims should be considered a criminal offence by the Bishop of Beauvais? As regards the question of her submission to the Church, Joan of Arc replied, when asked if she would submit to its will, in these words: 'You speak to me of the "Church Militant" and of the "Church Triumphant." I do not understand the signification of those terms; but I wish to submit myself to the Church as all good Christians should do.' What more could be required of her than this entire submission to the Church? She had made that answer to the doctors and clergy at Poitiers, and it had entirely satisfied those men. What Joan of Arc had a clear right not to do was to submit herself to her arch-enemy the Bishop of Beauvais. When she asked what Cauchon and his judges called the 'Church Militant,' she was told it consisted of the Pope and the prelates below him. She thereupon exclaimed she would willingly appear before him, but that she would not submit to the judgment of her enemies, and particularly not to Cauchon. 'In saying this,' adds M. Wallon, 'she displayed her usual courageous spirit. How eagerly had she,' he remarks (when told that if she would submit herself to the Council then sitting at Bale, where she would find some judges of her party among the English), 'appealed to be allowed to bring her case before that Council; and it will be remembered how Cauchon cursed the lawyer who had brought forward the suggestion during the trial.' On that occasion escaped from the prisoner's lips the cry which showed how well she knew the unscrupulousness of her judges. On learning that her wish to appeal to the Council of Bale by Cauchon's order was not to appear in that day's report of the trial, she said, 'You write down what is against me, but you will not write what is favourable to me.' Along with the twelve articles, Cauchon enclosed a letter to the lawyers in Paris asking for their opinion on what he calls the facts submitted to them, 'whether they do not appear to be contrary to the orthodox faith, to the Scriptures, and to the Church of Rome, and whether the learned members of the Church and doctors do not consider such things as stated in these articles as scandalous, dangerous to civil order, injurious and adverse to public morals.' In every way Cauchon's letter was worthy of its author.

  On the 12th of April a meeting under the presidency of Erard Emenyart, consisting of a score of lawyers and clergy, was held in the chapel of the archiepiscopal palace. At this meeting, with scarcely a dissentient voice, it was voted that Joan of Arc had by her deeds and her expressed opinions proved herself schismatical and strongly tainted with heresy. A second meeting took place in the same building on the following day, attended by some more Church functionaries. Some of these suggested that the prisoner should be promptly handed over to the secular arm--if she refuses still to renounce her errors--and if she acknowledges them, her fate will then be to be imprisoned for life, and given for nourishment 'the bread of sorrows and the water of anguish.' Eleven advocates--all belonging to Rouen--however, added the following clause, that the latter should be her punishment, 'provided that her revelations do not come from God.' But with the fear of Cauchon before them, they added to this clause that the revelations coming from such a source seems hardly probable, and they appeal to the bachelors in theology to set them right on that head. The Bishop of Lisieux, who had already given as his reason for not believing that Joan of Arc's mission could be Heaven-inspired the fact of the low station from which she came, now repeated the same absurdity on this occasion. There were others who preferred delaying their verdict until the decision arrived at by the University of Paris had been made known. A number of the Churchmen belonging to the Chapter of the Cathedral of Rouen hesitated, divided between two opinions, for and against the Maid, and of these only twenty put in an appearance when summoned by Cauchon to meet on the 13th of April. They were threatened and bullied by the Bishop to come in stronger numbers on the next day, when they attended to the number of thirty-one, but could not be prevailed on to give a definite opinion until the answer arrived from the University--which ultimatum Cauchon had to take with as much grace as he could. While these things were taking place, Joan of Arc fell ill--worn out probably by her long and harsh imprisonment, by the mental as well as physical torment she must have undergone during those weeks of cross-questioning and endless browbeating. Her jailers were more alarmed about her condition than she was herself, for were she to die a natural death, half the moral effect her enemies counted on obtaining by giving her the death of a sorceress and heretic would be lost. Doctors were sent for--sent by the Cardinal of Winchester and Warwick. When asked what ailed her she said that her illness had commenced after eating a fish that had been sent her by the Bishop of Beauvais. Warwick is said to have had the brutality to tell the doctors that her life must be saved at all hazards, for she had to die by the hands of the executioners. The doctors ordered her to be bled, and her naturally strong constitution soon restored her to health. During the days of the weakness following her illness, Cauchon, thinking probably that more might be then wrung from her than when well, came to see her. This was on the 18th of April. He went to the dungeon accompanied by the Vice-Inquisitor and half-a-dozen judges, and the following charitable exhortation, as the chronicler styles it, took place.

'We have come,' began Cauchon, 'to you with charitable and amiable intentions, to console you in your sickness. You will remember, Joan, how you have been questioned on various matters relating to the faith, and you know the answers you made. Knowing your ignorance relating to such matters, we are willing to send learned and well-versed men in such matters.' Then turning to the lawyers and others present, the Bishop continued: 'We exhort you to give Joan profitable counsel on the obligations which appertain to the true doctrine of the faith, and to the furtherance of the safety and welfare of her body and soul. 'Joan,' continued Cauchon, 'if there be any one else you wish to consult in this matter, we are ready to send for such in order that they may aid you. We are men of the Church, ever ready to aid those in need of advice good for the soul as well as the body, and ready to benefit you or any of your own kith, or ourselves. We should gladly give you daily such to advise you. In a word, we are ready, under the circumstances, to aid you, as does the Church itself, ever ready to help all such who will willingly come to her. But beware to act against our advice and exhortation. For if you still should refuse to submit yourself to us, we shall abandon you. Judge then of the peril you lie in in that case. It is this peril which we hope to prevent you from falling into with all our strength and all our affection.'

To this Mephistophelean address Joan of Arc made the following reply: 'I render you my best thanks for what you have said respecting the salvation of my soul; and it seems to me, seeing the illness I am now suffering, that I am in danger of dying. If this is to happen, God's will be done. I will only ask you to allow me to confess, and to partake of the Blessed Sacrament, and that my body may be laid in holy ground.'

Cauchon replied as follows: 'If you wish to receive the Sacraments of the Church you must confess yourself like a good Catholic, and you must also submit yourself to the Church. If you persevere in not doing so, you cannot obtain what you desire, except that for Penitence, which we are always ready to administer.'

Joan wearily said to this: 'I have then nothing more to say.'

The Bishop, however, had no wish that the interview should end thus, and continued: 'The greater your danger of now dying is, the greater reason have you to amend your life; if you do not submit yourself to the Church, then you will not obtain the privilege of a Catholic to its Sacraments.'

To this she answered: 'If I die here in prison, I trust my body will be placed in consecrated earth. If you refuse me this favour, I can but appeal to my Saviour!'

'You said,' quoth Cauchon, 'during the trial that if you had done or said anything that was against our Christian faith you could not support it!'

'I refer myself,' said Joan, 'to the answer I then made, and to our Lord!'

'You said,' continued the Bishop, 'that you had received many revelations both from God and from the saints. Suppose, then, that now some worthy person were to appear, declaring that they had received a revelation from God about your deeds, would you believe that person?'

To this the prisoner replied: 'There is not a Christian on earth, who, coming to me and saying that he came by such revelation, I should not know whether to believe or not, for I should know whether he were true or false by Saint Catherine and Saint Margaret.'

'But,' said Cauchon, 'do you imagine then that God is not able to reveal to some one besides yourself things that you may be ignorant about?'

Joan answered: 'Without a sign, I should not believe man or woman.'

Then Cauchon asked Joan if she believed in the holy Scriptures?

'You know that I do,' she answered.

Then the Bishop again returned to the question whether or not the prisoner consented to submit herself to the Church Militant, by which the Church Temporal should be understood.

Now, as before, Joan of Arc's answer was unchanged.

'Whatever,' she said, 'may happen to me, I shall neither do nor say anything further than that I have already declared during the trial.'

In vain all the venerable doctors present exhorted the prisoner to make her submission; they quoted Scripture, chapter and verse, to her (Matt. xviii.), without obtaining any more success than the Bishop had done.

As they were leaving the prison one of these 'venerable doctors' hissed to Joan: 'If you refuse to submit to the Church, the Church will abandon you as if you were a Saracen.'

To this Joan of Arc replied: 'I am a good Christian--a Christian born and baptized--and a Christian I shall die.'

Before Cauchon left his victim he made one further attempt to obtain a decided answer from Joan of Arc, this time making use of a bait which he thought must catch her--namely, permission to receive the Communion: 'As,' he said, 'you desire the Eucharist, will you, if you are allowed to do so, submit yourself to the Church?'

To this offer Joan answered: 'As to that submission I can give no other answer than that I have already given you. I love God; Him I serve, as a good Christian should. Were I able I would help the Church with all my strength.'

'But,' said Cauchon, 'if we were to order a grand procession to restore your health, then would you not submit yourself?'

'I only request,' she answered, 'that the Church and all good Catholics will pray for me.'

Some of the judges had suggested that, in a more public place than in her prison, Joan of Arc should be again admonished relating to the crimes of which she was accused; and Cauchon accordingly summoned a public meeting of the judges for the 2nd of May, to be held in a chamber near the Great Hall.

On that day sixty-two judges were present. Cauchon took care that the actual charges contained in the twelve articles which had been sent to the University should not be read in the presence of the prisoner, and told her that she had only been summoned in order to receive another admonition before a larger assemblage than had as yet met.

In his opening allocution he told his audience that the private admonition had been unattended with good results, that Joan had refused to submit herself to the Church, and that he had accordingly invited to the present meeting a learned doctor of theology, namely, John de Chatillon, archdeacon of Evreux, whose eloquence he doubted not would have a beneficial effect upon the stubbornness of the prisoner.

On Joan being led into the room, the Bishop admonished her to listen to what Chatillon would now lay before her, and to agree to what he would advise. If she would not do so, he added, she would place herself in jeopardy, both as to her body and as to her soul.

Chatillon then took up his parable, which was to the effect that all faithful Christians must conform to the tenets of the Church; and that he trusted she would do so to all that the doctors lay and spiritual there present expected her.

The Archdeacon held a digest of his sermon in his hand. Seeing this, Joan of Arc requested him to read his book, after which, she said, she would make her answer.

The speech, or sermon, that he then delivered was an exhaustive examination of the twelve articles, brought under six heads, but much altered and garbled.

In the first place, he admonished her of not having given a full account of her apparitions to the Church through her judges; secondly, he told her of her culpability in insisting on retaining her male attire; thirdly, of her wickedness in asserting that she committed no crime in retaining that dress; fourthly, her sin in holding as true revelations that could only lead the people into error; fifthly, that she had, owing to these revelations, done deeds displeasing to the Divine will; and lastly, that she was committing a sin in treating the apparitions as holy, when she was not certain whether they did not come from evil spirits. When Chatillon said that by not conforming to the article 'Sanctam Ecclesiam,' she placed herself in the power of the Church to condemn her to the flames, and to be burnt as a heretic, she answered boldly:

'I will not say aught else than that I have already spoken; and were I even to see the fire I should say the same!'

After this answer in the minutes of that day's trial is written by the clerk in the margin of the vellum:

'Superba responsio!'

That was a testimony of admiration which neither the fears of persecution nor of superstition could prevent from appearing.

Nothing more was to be obtained from the prisoner's lips than this declaration, either by private or public examinations. This being so, Cauchon bethought him what further cruelty could be employed to force the prisoner to give way, and the barbarous scheme of torture was decided on.

The only portion of the old castle of Rouen that has survived Time, war, revolutions, and rebuilding (although partially restored), is a massive high tower, built of white stone, called the Tower of Joan of Arc. This is not the tower of the castle which contained the heroine's dungeon, but it has always been traditionally regarded as that in which, on the 9th of May, Joan of Arc was led to where her judges intended, by fear or by the infliction of bodily torment, to oblige her to make the confession which she had so steadily and for so long a time refused. The lower portion of this tower only is ancient, for from about its centre to the top is a restoration.

The chamber to which Joan of Arc was led, and where the instruments of torture and the executioners were waiting, is probably that on the ground floor, and is but little changed from what it was on that May morning in the year of grace 1431.

In that dark stone chamber with its groined roof, besides the prisoner, were present Cauchon, with the Vice-Inquisitor, the Abbot of Saint Corneille of Compiegne, William Erard, Andrew Marguerie, Nicolas de Venderes, John Massieu, William Haiton, Aubert Morel, and the infamous Loiseleur. Ranged round the circular walls were placed the instruments of torture, and men skilled in their use were ready at hand.

'Joan,' said Cauchon, who had now dropped his hypocritical semblance of sympathy, which he had assumed when interrogating the prisoner in her cell, 'I command you to tell the truth. In your examination many and various points have been touched on, about which you refused to answer, or, when you did so, answered untruthfully. Of this we have certain proof. These points will now be read to you.'

What was then read was probably a summary of the articles of impeachment.

Cauchon then continued: 'If, Joan, you now refuse to speak the truth, you will be put to the torture. You see before you the instruments which are prepared, and by them stand the executioners, who are ready to do their office at our command. You will be tortured in order that you may be led into the way of truth, and for the salvation of your body and soul, which you by your lies have exposed to so great a peril.'

It was at this terrible juncture that Joan showed her indomitable spirit more clearly than at any moment since her capture. In front of her lay the rack upon which, at a signal from Cauchon, her limbs would be wrenched asunder; but her reply, as given in the minutes written by the clerk who was present, bears the ring of a courage superior to all the terrors which confronted her.

'Even,' she said, 'if you tear me limb from limb, and even if you kill me, I will not tell you anything further. And even were I forced to do so, I should afterwards declare that it was only because of the torture that I had spoken differently.'

That was an answer which sums up the whole folly and crime of obtaining evidence by means of torture, and recalls Galileo's famous phrase when in a somewhat similar situation.

Cauchon then again ordered Joan to tell them of her revelations, and asked her if she had again sought counsel from her voices.

She had, answered Joan.

'And have they,' asked the Bishop, 'foretold what will now happen?'

'I asked them,' answered Joan of Arc, 'if I should be burnt, and they answered: "Abide by your Lord and He will aid you."'

There is little more than the above recorded of what took place, but it is probable that Joan, who had as yet hardly recovered from her illness, was, from fear of her dying under the torture, not subjected to it. At any rate, that additional horror was not to be laid on the consciences of the already heavily burthened judges of the Maid.

It appears, however, that these men had not altogether given up the idea of carrying out this barbarity, so congenial to such a man as Cauchon and to his friend the Inquisitor; for a meeting was summoned by Cauchon at his house three days after Joan had been brought face to face with the torture apparatus, at which the question was discussed as to whether it should not after all be used.

Thirteen judges met the Bishop and the Inquisitor to discuss the question. Of these the following were against applying torture: Maitres Roussel, Venderes, Marguerie, Erard, Barbier, Gastinel, Coppequesne, Ledoux, De la Pierre, Haiton, and Lemaistre. One of these, Erard, remarked that it was unnecessary to torture the prisoner seeing that, as he expressed it, 'they had already sufficient evidence to condemn her to death without putting her to torment.' But Morel de Courcelles, and Loiseleur were in favour that it should be made use of. Surely the names of these men deserve to be held in execration, and placed by the side of Cauchon's in the historic pillory of everlasting infamy.

Meanwhile the University of Paris were deliberating upon their answer to the twelve articles. This body met on the 29th of April, within the convent of Saint Bernard. The ancient building, in which the University held many notable conclaves when even Popes were judged by the doctors of Paris, still exists, but it has been transformed into an oil warehouse. John de Troyes, senior of the Faculty of Theology, was the spokesman, and read the decisions of the faculty on each of the twelve articles. It is unnecessary to go through the long verbiage of abuse and blasphemy with which these theologians thought it their duty to bespatter Joan of Arc.

On every head these reverend seigneurs condemned her. After De Troyes had finished his reading of the opinions and the judgment, Guerold de Boissel read the deliberations of the Faculty of Decrees upon the six points of accusation. 'If this woman,' so ran the rede, 'was in her right mind when she made affirmation of the propositions contained in the twelve articles, one may say in the manner of counsel and of doctrine, and to speak charitably, first, that she is schismatic in separating herself from obedience to the Church; secondly, that she is out of the pale of the law in contradicting the article "Unam Sanctam Ecclesiam Catholicam"; thirdly, apostate, for having cut short her hair, which was given her by God to hide her head with, and also in having abandoned the dress of a woman for that of a man; fourthly, vicious and a soothsayer, for saying, without showing miracles, that she is sent by God, as was Moses and John the Baptist; fifthly, rebel to the faith, by remaining under the anathema framed by the canons of the Church, and by not receiving the Sacraments of the Church at the season set apart by the Church, in order not to have to cease wearing the dress of a man; and, sixthly, blasphemous in saying that she knows she will be received into Paradise. Therefore, if after being charitably warned she refuses to re-enter the Catholic faith, and thereby give satisfaction, she shall be given over to the secular judges, and meet with the punishment due to her crimes.'

And the University of Paris in solemn conclave ratified the above judgment. The University also sent Cauchon a letter of commendation, in which he was held up to the general admiration as a faithful pastor, zealous in good works, on whom the University trusted that the Almighty would, on the day of His manifestation, bestow an imperishable crown of glory.

Such were the sentiments of the most erudite, most pious, and most eminent school of learning existing in the capital of France. On the 19th of May Cauchon summoned yet another gathering of Joan's judges in the archiepiscopal palace at

Rouen. Fifty of them attended. After some discussion, during which a few of the learned men present expressed their opinion that Joan of Arc should be at once handed over to the secular arm, it was decided that the prisoner should again be brought before them to be what they were pleased to call 'charitably admonished.' Accordingly, four days after, on the 23rd of May, in a chamber near Joan of Arc's dungeon, another meeting was held. On this occasion a canon of Rouen, named Peter Morice, was ordered to question the prisoner.

He commenced by delivering a long lecture, in which he recapitulated the twelve articles, and wound up his oration by imploring Joan to submit herself to the Church Militant, and threatening her with the loss of body and soul in this world and the next if she still refused to do so.

Joan of Arc was as unmoved and as firm when thus threatened as she had been when placed before the instruments of torture, and she replied:--

'If I were to see the fire itself, the stake, and the executioner ready to light the pile, and were I in the midst of the flames, I should not say anything else than what I have already spoken during the trial, and this is my determination, even unto my death!'

There is some probability for believing that, during the following evening after this last meeting of Joan of Arc and her judges, Loiseleur gained admittance to the prisoner, and, under the disguise of a friendly and sympathetic priest, promised Joan that if she would conform to the wishes of the judges, she should be taken out of the prison she now lay in and the custody of the English, and transferred to prisons belonging to the Church.

Poor Joan's chief desire was that she might be set free from the hands of the English. Be this as it may, there is no authority given for this idea of Loiseleur having probed her on this point; and Wallon, in his history of the Maid, makes no allusion to such an interview, and only states that John Beaupere went in the morning of the 24th to the prison, and he was soon followed there by Nicolas Loiseleur, who vehemently urged on Joan to comply with the demands which the judges had made.

Nothing had been neglected to give the greatest solemnity to the cruel farce which Cauchon had prepared to be now enacted--a solemnity by which the Bishop hoped to degrade Joan of Arc in the eyes of the people. It was that of obliging the prisoner to make a public apology and recantation of all her deeds--a declaration in fact to be made by her in the eyes of the whole world that all she had undertaken and accomplished had been through and by the aid of evil spirits.

By this stroke the Bishop hoped to show to France that its heroine, instead of being a sainted and holy maid sent by God to deliver her country from the invader, was, by her own open and public confession, proved to be an emanation from Satan--a being abhorrent in the eyes of God and man. By this device, Cauchon hoped also to deal a blow to Charles, for when once it became known that his servant and saviour was a creature in league with the fiends, all the works done through her influence, and by her prowess, including his coronation, would also be proved to have been accomplished by the powers of darkness, and therefore deeds abhorrent to all good Catholics throughout his realm.

The place chosen for the stage on which Joan of Arc was to abjure before the eyes of Rouen--and through Rouen the rest of France--her deeds and her words, was the cemetery in front of that most beautiful of all Gothic fanes--the Church of Saint Ouen.

Adjacent to its southern wall the exquisitely carved portal named the Marmousets, then as now rich in statuary of royal and imperial benefactors of the Church, looks down upon what is the entrance to a fair public garden. In the fifteenth century this space was used as a place of burial.

Here, arranged with a view to dramatic effect, were placed two huge wooden scaffolds, or rather platforms, which faced one another. Upon one of these sat the Bishop of Beauvais in state. He had on his right hand the Prince Cardinal of Winchester, great-uncle of the child-king Henry VI., with other notabilities of the Church; the Bishops of Norwich, of Noyon, and of Therouenne; the Vice-Inquisitor, eight abbots, and a large number of friars and doctors, clerical and lay--in fact all those who had attended the trials of the Maid of Orleans during the two preceding months. Upon the opposite platform stood Joan of Arc, a crowd of lawyers and priests about her. Here, too, stood Loiseleur close by the prisoner; he never ceased urging her to conform to the commands of the clergy about her.

A vast throng of the town's-people gathered below, and the place was all in a turmoil. A seething mob had followed the Maid from her prison to the cemetery, which, already full, now held with difficulty the fresh press of people who accompanied Joan of Arc and her guards to the purlieus of the Church of Saint Ouen.

William Erard had been appointed by Cauchon to preach in this 'terrible comedy,' as Michelet calls this farce of the Maid's abjuration. For text the monk selected the fifteenth chapter of Saint John's gospel: 'The branch,' etc. Erard showed in his discourse how Joan had fallen from one sin into another, till she had at length separated herself from the Church. To a long string of abuse about herself Joan of Arc listened with perfect patience; but the preacher, not content with hurling his invectives at the prisoner, began to attack her King for having listened to Joan's advice, by which conduct the King had, Erard said, also incurred the crime of heresy.

This attack on Charles roused the indignation of the Maid. Turning on the monk, without a moment's thought of her own situation, and the fresh danger she exposed herself to, the noble girl exclaimed: 'By my faith, and with all respect to you, I dare to affirm on my peril that the King of this realm is the noblest of Christians, and no one has greater love for the Faith and Church than my King!'

'Silence her!' shrieked the preacher, beside himself with rage at finding that these few words from the lips of Joan of Arc had destroyed all the effect of his eloquence on that vast crowd, whose sympathy must have been now strongly shown towards the glorious victim before them.

Again summoned to submit to the Church, Joan said: 'I have answered on that point already to my judges. I call upon them to send an account of all my actions to the Holy Father at Rome, to whom after God I submit myself.'

This was not what Cauchon wished his victim to express, for one of the charges that he had made against her was her refusal to submit to the Pope. He therefore changed the subject, and asked Joan of Arc whether she acknowledged that there were any things evil among those deeds she had committed or said.

'As to my deeds and sayings,' she answered, 'I have done them by the command of God.'

'Then you admit,' said the Bishop, 'that the King and others have sometimes urged you to act as you have done?'

'As to my words and actions,' she answered, 'I make no one, and particularly not the King, responsible. If any wrong has been committed, it is I who am to blame, and not another.'

'But,' said Cauchon, 'those acts and words of yours which have been found evil by the judges, will you recant them?'

'I submit them,' said Joan, 'to God and our Holy Father the Pope.'

'The bishops,' continued Cauchon, 'are the judges in their dioceses, therefore you must submit to the Church as your judges have determined that you shall do.'

Joan still refused, and the Bishop then began to read the sentence condemning her to death as a heretic.

Now arose a great uproar among the clergy and others on the platforms and among the crowd beneath. Loiseleur and Massieu urged her to abjure; the former promising that if she consented she would, after abjuring, be taken from her English jailers and placed in keeping of the clergy. In the midst of the hubbub Erard produced a parchment scroll, on which, he told Joan, were written the different accusations against her, which she had only to sign with her mark to be saved. All about this abjuration was a mesh of confusion to the mind of Joan. Massieu told her she need but make a mark on the parchment before her to be delivered: if not--and he pointed down to a grim figure near the foot of the stage they were on, where stood the headsman with cart and assistants, ready to draw her to the stake.

'Abjure!' cried Erard and Massieu, 'or you will be taken and burnt.'

Even Joan of Arc's courage failed at that sight, and all the woman in her nature asserted itself.

'Do what I tell you,' cried Loiseleur; 'abjure and put on woman's dress, and all will yet be well.'

The text of the abjuration was then hurriedly read, Joan of Arc following it, and repeating the words, the sense of which she had no time to understand. She spoke the words, it is said, as one in a dream. Some said she did this mockingly, for she was observed to smile once or twice; but the poor soul's spirit was crushed, and doubtless the whole scene was to her like an evil dream--the poor broken-down body could not discriminate what words she was forced to repeat. A troubled, horrible dream must that have seemed to the hapless maiden, standing on that scaffold, with all the shouting mob about, and all her deadly enemies at hand. She made her mark on the parchment--a little cross--and the deed was done.

In the recantation, or abjuration, thus obtained from Joan of Arc, the twelve articles were included, with all their abuse set down. Thus was Joan obliged by her signature to declare that all her visions and voices were false and from evil spirits;

also that she had been guilty of transgressing laws divine in having worn her hair cut short and the dress of a man; also in having caused bloodshed; also in having idolatrously invoked evil spirits; also in having treated God and His sacraments with contempt; and, besides all this, of having acted schismatically, and of having fallen foul of the Church: all of which crimes and errors she now abjured, and humbly submitted herself to the will of the Church and its ordinances. She promised with her abjuration not to relapse, and called on Saint Peter, the Pope, as well as the Bishop of Beauvais and other of her judges, to keep her word.

Not content with having inveigled Joan of Arc into signing this farrago of blasphemous nonsense, her judges, it seems, added fraud to their crime by reading to the prisoner a different recantation from that to which they had forced her to sign her mark. The one she marked contained only six lines, and it did not take longer to read these few lines, an eye-witness afterwards asserted, than it does to repeat the 'Paternoster'; whereas the one produced after the ceremony of the abjuration filled several sides. But in an act of such infamy as this of having cheated Joan of Arc not only into signing a recantation of her life-work, but of confessing to her existence having been one long series of superstitious and criminal workings with the spirits of evil, it matters very little whether she signed a longer or a shorter list of falsehoods invented by her persecuting judges.

While these things were taking place upon the platform on which Joan was bullied into signing this abjuration, the English and their faction in the crowd below began to fear that their victim would escape them; they had not grasped the astuteness of the French prelate, who was ready to hand his prisoner over to them directly he had obtained this recantation from her hand. Cauchon was, however, obliged to keep them waiting until he had got that by which he hoped to destroy Joan of Arc's fame, and at the same time, and by the same deed, to retain in his possession a formidable weapon by which he thought to weaken the cause of the French monarch.

Cauchon may well have felt on that afternoon that what he had done for the English cause merited as his reward the coveted archbishopric of Rouen. There remained but one further act for him to play in this drama before he quitted his platform. Rising from among his brother bishops he read a list of the crimes committed by the prisoner, and announced that, as Joan had now, owing to her abjuration of her sins, re-entered into the fold of the Church, she was absolved by him from her excommunication. However, he added, as she had sinned so grievously against God and the Church, he, for the sake of her soul's welfare, condemned her to perpetual imprisonment--'to the water of sorrow, and the bread of anguish,' so that she might repent of her faults, and cease ever to commit any more.

Then, in spite of the promises made to her of being placed in the charge of the clergy, Cauchon ordered that Joan should be taken back to her former prison.

Warwick is said to have displayed anger at this termination of the proceedings. Observing this, one of the judges pacified him by assuring him that Joan should not be allowed to escape her fate: 'Do not fear, my lord,' he said; 'you will catch her yet.'

That evening the Vice-Inquisitor, accompanied by Loiseleur, Thomas de Courcelles, Isambard de la Pierre, and a few other of the judges who had taken part in the proceedings that day at Saint Ouen, visited the prisoner. Their object in going to her was to insist upon her changing her man's dress, with which demand she now had to comply. That occurred on Thursday night, and on the Sunday following a rumour was spread abroad that Joan of Arc had discarded the woman's dress, and had again put on male dress.

Although, during the last days of the heroine's life, it is most difficult to gather anything authentic as to her treatment in the prison, we are led to understand, by the least untrustworthy testimony, that what happened in the interval between Thursday night and the following Sunday was as follows.

The soldiers placed in charge of Joan after her recantation and her return to the prison had rendered her existence a long martyrdom; and there is reason to believe that on her discarding her man's dress these ruffians attempted to violate the prisoner: so, sooner than suffer this, although she knew that to return to her former dress would be equivalent to meeting certain death, she did not hesitate to save her maidenhood at the exposure of her life.

Michelet, in his history of the Maid, quotes from the deposition of one of the officials--Massieu, who saw much of Joan of Arc in those last days--the statement that on the morning of Trinity Sunday, on waking, she asked the soldiers to leave her alone for a few moments while she dressed; that one of the men removed her woman's clothes, and in place substituted the dress of a man; and that, in order not to be naked, she was obliged to put on the latter.

Be this as it may, on the following morning, Cauchon, followed by several of his creatures, returned to the prison, in order that he might see and show to others that his victim had been entrapped at last. 'We have come,' he said to the prisoner, 'to find out the state of your soul, and we find you, in despite of our command, and despite of your promise to renounce this man's dress, again thus attired. Tell us the reason why you have dared again to wear these clothes.'

Joan's answer was that she preferred that dress to the other, and that, being placed among men, it was better that she should wear it than the dress of a woman. Although not placed in the judicial record of this interview, Manchon adds in his account of the proceedings on that day, that Joan of Arc also said that she had returned to wearing her male attire, feeling safer when in that dress than when she was dressed in woman's clothes. This seems to us an evident avowal that she had to resist the brutality of the men placed over her in the dungeon. Massieu also adds to Manchon's testimony that he knew Joan was unable to protect herself against attempts made to violate her. Her legs were chained to the wood with which her pallet bed was framed, and this chain was again fixed to a large beam about six feet long, and locked with a padlock; so that the poor creature could hardly move. To the above testimony of these two men, Isambard de la Pierre adds his. He states that when Cauchon came to the Maid's dungeon she bore all the traces of having undergone a violent struggle, 'being all in tears, and so bruised and outraged (outragee) that he (Isambard) could not help feeling pity for her.'

But the strongest testimony of all is that of the priest, Martin Ladvenu, who heard her confession on the eve of her death, and he confirms Isambard's statement entirely. He even adds that not only had Joan of Arc to suffer from the brutality of the soldiery placed about her, but that a ***millourt d'Angleterre*** had acted as shamefully as these men towards her.

Although Michelet and other French writers have naturally not allowed this 'Millourt' (which, by the way, is quite as correct a form of spelling that title as the better known 'Milor') to escape the branding he deserves for his attempted villainy, it is but fair to add that Isambard de la Pierre, as well as Manchon, qualify his conduct as that not of a would-be violator, but of a tempter--a not inconsiderable difference in the scale of infamy.

To return to Cauchon and Joan of Arc.

'But,' said the Bishop, 'are you not aware you have now no right to wear such a dress?'

Joan answered that she had been misled into believing that if she wore the woman's dress she would be allowed to hear Mass and to communicate, and to be, she added, 'delivered from these chains.'

'But,' replied Cauchon, 'have you not abjured, and promised never to take to wearing this dress again?'

'I would prefer to die,' she answered, 'than to remain on a prisoner here. But if I were allowed to go to the Mass, and these chains were taken off me, and if I was placed in some other prison where some woman could be near me, then I should do all that is required of me by the Church.'

In all Joan of Arc's answers it should be noticed that she never, in spite of the terrible sufferings she endured, and the gross barbarities inflicted on her, in any single instance ever made any complaint of her treatment. There is something superhuman in this utter absence of any shade of vindictiveness, when one thinks that, by a few words, she might have saved herself from much of what she had to suffer. Never once did she blame even those who had deceived, insulted, and ill-treated her; her life was one beautiful example, full of divine charity and forgiveness.

Cauchon, to make doubly sure of completing his work, then asked Joan: 'Have you, since last Thursday, heard the voices of Saint Catherine and Saint Margaret?'

'Yes,' she answered.

'And,' continued the Bishop, 'what did they say?'

'They told me of the great sorrow they felt for the great treason to which I have been led, by my abjuring and revoking my deeds in order to save my life, and that by so doing I have lost my soul.'

On the margin of the original document of the MSS. of this examination, written in the prison, the original of which is in the National Library in Paris, we find alongside of this answer of Joan of Arc's the following words: 'Responsio mortifera.' Indeed it was an answer of deadliest import; for Joan in asserting that her voices had again spoken to her, and in saying that she had committed a mortal sin by recanting her deeds, had thrown away the only plank of safety left her.

It seems to us evident, however, that Joan of Arc was now quite eager and willing to meet the worst that her enemies could inflict upon her: death itself must now have seemed more tolerable than the daily death she was undergoing in her prison.

'Did your voices urge you to resist giving way about the recantation?' questioned the Bishop.

'My voices,' Joan said, 'told me as I stood on the platform before the people that I should answer the preacher with boldness.'

'Did he not,' said Cauchon, 'speak the truth?'

'No,' she answered, 'he was a false preacher; and he accused me of having done things which I never did.'

'But,' then said Cauchon, 'do you mean to tell us that you still persist in saying that you have been sent by God?'

To which Joan replied that that was still her belief.

'Then,' continued the Bishop, 'you deny that to which you swore on oath only last Thursday?'

'My voices,' said Joan, 'have told me since then that I had committed a bad deed in saying that I had not done the things which I have done!'

'Then,' continued the Bishop, with eagerness, 'you retract your abjuration?'

'It was,' said Joan of Arc, 'from the fear of being burnt that I retracted what I had done; but I never intended to deny or revoke my voices.'

'But then,' said Cauchon, 'are you now no longer afraid of being burnt?'

'I had rather die than endure any longer what I have now to undergo.'

And with these broken-hearted words of the sufferer ended this long mockery of a trial, so patiently endured during three wearyful months by the martyr Maid.

On quitting the prison, Cauchon met Lord Warwick among some Englishmen in the outer court of the castle. They were clamouring that the execution of Joan of Arc should be soon carried out. The Bishop accosted the Earl with a smile of triumph, and said to him in English:--

'You can dine now with a good appetite. We have caught her at last!'

CHAPTER VI.
MARTYRDOM.

The next day, the 29th of May, Cauchon summoned a large number of prelates and doctors--forty-two in all--to meet him at the archiepiscopal chapel, where he recounted to them all the circumstances of his late interview with the prisoner. He told them how he had found Joan, in spite of her abjuration, again dressed as a man, and of her having reaffirmed all that she had so recently abjured regarding her voices and apparitions. When he had concluded, Cauchon took the opinion of those around him. Without one dissentient voice, they all affirmed that she should be handed over to the secular arm--i.e., burnt. The deliberation had not taken long, and, after thanking the company, the Bishop made out a formal order by which Joan was summoned at eight o'clock on the next morning to the old market-place, there to be delivered into the hands of the civil judge, and by him to be handed over to those of the executioners. 'We conclude,' said the Bishop, as he dismissed the meeting, 'that Joan shall be treated as a relapsed heretic, for this appears to us right and proper in the sight of law and justice.'

Early in the morning of Wednesday, the 30th of May--a date which should be held sacred in France as that of the martyrdom of her who through all time must be her country's greatest glory--two priests (Martin Ladvenu and John Toutmouille) were sent by the Bishop's order to the prisoner to tell her that her last day on earth had come. Toutmouille describes, with some pathos, the manner in which Joan of Arc received the terrible news. She, he tells us, at first wept bitterly, and said she would sooner be beheaded seven times than suffer such a death as that of burning. She recalled with pain the promises made by Cauchon to her--that after she had abjured she would be taken to the prison of the Church, for then, she said, this cruel death would not have befallen her; and she called upon God, 'the omnipotent and just Judge,' to take pity on her. While she thus lamented her fate, Cauchon entered the dungeon. Turning on him, she cried: 'I lay my death at your door; for had you placed me in the prison of the Church, this cruel death would not have befallen me, and I make you responsible to God for my death.'

Then, turning away from the Bishop, she appeared more calm, and, addressing one of the judges who had followed Cauchon into the prison, exclaimed: 'Master Peter'--the man's name was Peter Maurice--'where shall I be this evening?'

'Have you not good hope in God's mercy?' he answered.

'Yes,' said Joan; 'and by His grace I hope to be in Paradise.'

Cauchon and the others having left her alone with Martin Ladvenu, she made her confession to him, and when that was finished she begged that the Sacrament might be administered to her. Without Cauchon's leave Ladvenu did not dare to obtain this supreme consolation for the martyr.

He despatched a messenger to the Bishop, who, after consulting with some of the clergy, gave his permission. In the meanwhile, the city had heard that the day of the Maid of Orleans' execution had come, and the people crowded about the neighbourhood of the castle. In spite of the English soldiery, the people did not conceal their grief and dismay on learning that the heroine was so soon to perish. The Eucharist was brought into the prison, but without the usual accompaniments of candle, stole, and surplice. These 'maimed rights' raised the indignation of the priest Martin, and he indignantly refused to proceed with the ceremony until lights and stole were brought. During the time in which Joan of Arc was receiving the Sacrament, those persons who had been admitted within the castle recited the litany for the departing soul, and never had the mournful invocation for the dying, the supplication of the solemn chant, 'Kyrie eleison! Christe eleison!' been raised from a more tragic place, or on a more heart-stirring occasion. Outside, in the street, and all around the prison gates, knelt the weeping people, fervently praying, and earnestly invoking the Almighty and His saints for her who was about to lay down her young life in their behalf. 'Christ have pity! Saint Margaret have pity! Pray for her, all ye saints, archangels, and blessed martyrs, pray for her! Saints and angels intercede for her! From Thy wrath, good Lord, deliver her! O, Lord God, save her! Have mercy on her, we beseech thee, good Lord!' The poor, helpless people had nothing but their prayers to give Joan of Arc; but these we may believe were not unavailing.

There are few more pathetic events recorded in history than this weeping, helpless, praying crowd, holding their lighted candles, and kneeling, on the pavement, beneath the prison walls of the old fortress.

It was about nine o'clock when they placed on Joan of Arc a long white shirt, such as criminals wore at their execution, and on her head they set a mitre-shaped paper cap, on which the words 'heretic, relapsed, apostate, idolatress,' were written.

This was the head-dress which the victims of the Inquisition carried, and in which they were burnt.

When Joan of Arc was taken forth to die, there mounted with her on to the cart the two priests, Martin Ladvenu and Isambard. Eight hundred English troops lined the road by which the death-cart and its load passed from the castle to the old market-place; they were armed with staves and with axes. These soldiers, as the victim passed, fell into line behind the cart, and kept off with their staves the crowd, eager to show its sympathy for Joan.

Suddenly, when as yet the procession had gone but a short distance, a man pushed his way through the crowd and the soldiers, and threw himself at Joan of Arc's feet, imploring her forgiveness.

It was the priest Loiseleur, Joan's confessor and betrayer. Roughly thrown back by the men-at-arms, Loiseleur disappeared in the throng, but not before Joan had bestowed her pardon on him. On the old market-place--where now not a single building remains which witnessed the tragedy of that day--was a wide space, surrounded by picturesquely gabled and high-roofed houses, like those which still survive in the old Norman capital, and within a short distance of the churches of Saint Sauveur and Saint Michel, now destroyed. Two tribunes had been raised on either side of the square. Between this, placed high on a stage of masonry, stood the pile. A placard affixed in front of this pile bore a long inscription, beginning thus: 'Joan, known as the Maid' ... and ending with a cumbrous list of epithets, among which 'apostate' and 'schismatic' were the least abusive.

Pending the final act, a monk named Nicolas Midi was ordered by Cauchon to address the prisoner and those present. The Bishop's words have come down to us.

'For your admonition,' he began, 'and for the edification of all those present, a learned discourse will now be delivered by the distinguished doctor, Nicolas Midi';

and the distinguished doctor then took for his text, from the first Epistle of Saint Paul to the Corinthians, twelfth chapter, the words: 'If one member suffereth,' etc.

The gist of his sermon was to prove that it was necessary, in order to prevent others falling into sin, that the guilty member should be removed. Strange, indeed, how often the words of Scripture have been used and mis-used in excuse, or in vindication, of the most atrocious cruelties by so-called Christians, professing to preach the religion of mercy, of forgiveness, and of humanity.

The sermon being finished, the preacher addressed Joan of Arc in the following words: 'Joan, the Church, wishing to prevent infection, casts you from her. She no longer protects you. Depart in peace!'

Then Cauchon took up his text, which was to the effect that Joan, 'by renouncing her abjuration, had returned as the dog of Scripture did to its vomit; for which cause we, Peter, by the divine mercy Bishop of Beauvais, and brother John Lemaitre, vicar of the very reverend doctor John Graverent Inquisitor of the heretical evil [especially retained by Cauchon in the present case], have by a just judgment, declared you, Joan, commonly styled the Maid, fallen back into diverse errors and crimes, schismatical, idolatrous, and guilty of other sins in great number. For these causes we declare you fallen back into your former errors, and by the sentence of excommunication under which you were already found guilty we declare you to be heretical and relapsed; and we declare that you, as a decayed member, to prevent the contagion from spreading to others, are cast from the unity of the Church, and given over to the secular power. We reject, we cast you off, and we abandon you, praying that, beyond death and the mutilation of your limbs, the Church treats you with moderation.'

These last words were the usual formula used by the Inquisition when its victims were about to be committed to the flames. Joan of Arc meanwhile was praying fervently; and when Cauchon had finished speaking, she humbly begged those around her to pray for her. Her tears, her fervour, and her submission, overcame the feelings even of her judges.

Winchester was seen to weep, and a great wave of pity swept over the immense confused crowd; for her enemies as well as her friends among the people were all more or less under its influence.

In her prayers the heroine implored the Divine Mercy to pardon those from whom she had suffered so much. 'Pray for me in your churches,' she said to the priests--to those priests and to the Church that had deserted and condemned her; for in spite of all that she had endured at the hands of those Churchmen, Joan of Arc remained to the end as fervent and loyal a Churchwoman as she had been throughout her life.

One thing she missed. Turning to Massieu, she asked him if he had a cross. He had not, nor could one be found; but an Englishman broke his stave into two pieces, and these tied together formed a rude cross.

This cross Joan took, and placed it against her heart; but she still wanted a consecrated cross to be held before her while struggling in the flames, and this was at length obtained by the priest Isambard, who fetched one from the adjacent Church of Saint Sauveur.

Meanwhile the English soldiers began to grumble at the length of these preparations: 'Do they expect us to dine here?' they growled.

As soon as the cross from the church had been placed in her hands, she devoutly kissed it, invoking God and her saints to assist her in this the heaviest of her needs, when all human help had abandoned her.

The heroine appears to have been then seized by the English sergeants-at-arms, and given by them into the charge of the executioners; and while she was being led to the foot of the high pile of clay and wood--the instrument of her martyrdom--the men-at-arms surrounded and roughly handled their prisoner. The scene had become so poignant that many of the judges left their tribune, unable to endure the sight of that white-robed and helpless figure in the midst of the brutal soldiers hounding her on to her death. It must indeed have been a ghastly spectacle, even for men accustomed to scenes of savage brutality and cruelty. At length she was delivered from her tormentors, and, preceded by the executioner, she mounted the ladder, and was bound round the body by a chain attached to the stake.

The good priest, Isambard, closely followed her, and stood immediately beneath her, with the cross held and raised towards Joan, who but once removed her gaze from off it.

'Keep it,' she said to Isambard, 'keep it always before my eyes, till death.'

Then she took a last look around her--a last look on a world which had been so harsh and cruel a world to her, poor victim of all the powers of evil on this earth!

She looked but once on the surging crowd beneath, at the old timbered houses of the town, filled from basement to high-peaked roof, with thousands of its citizens. 'O, Rouen, Rouen!' she cried, 'must I die here? I have great fear lest you will suffer for my death.' And with that she put away from her all earthly things, and gave herself up to Heaven. In the interval the executioners had lighted the lower portion of the pile of wood, and the fire, fed by the pitch-covered fagots, mounted rapidly.

Joan of Arc gave a cry of terror, and called aloud for 'Water, holy water!' The body had for an instant conquered the spirit--but it was only for an instant.

At that moment Cauchon had the inconceivable and apparently devil-driven curiosity to approach the martyr, hoping, perhaps, that in the first terror at seeing the fire springing up to her, Joan of Arc would let fall some words of reproach against her King or her saints.

'Joan,' he cried through the crackling of the flames, 'I have come to exhort you for the last time.'

'I die through you,' she said, as she had said once before, and then she was allowed to die in peace, so far as Cauchon and his Church were concerned. For her all earthly things were now over. Till the last sign of life expired the eye-witnesses who have given us the fullest account of her last moments--the priests Isambard and Massieu--declared that she continued to call on her God and on her saints. Frequently through the blinding smoke and the fierce rush of flame her face looked that of a blessed saint uplifted and radiant.

With one loud cry of 'Jesus!' her head fell on her breast.

Thus came Joan of Arc to her glorious end.

There is a tradition that when the ashes of the martyr Maid were gathered to be cast into the Seine, the heart was found unconsumed--Cor cordium!

Many other traditions are related regarding her death, but none with much certainty. The executioner is said to have come later on that day to Isambard in an agony of grief. He confessed himself, and told Isambard that he felt Heaven would never pardon him for the part he had taken in killing a saint. The poor fellow's responsibility for her death was really not greater than that of the fagots and the flames which had destroyed her life. On Cauchon and his gang of judges, lay and clerical--on the University of Paris and the Catholic Church--on Winchester and the English, noble and simple, who had sold and bought the glorious Maid, the crime of her martyrdom will ever rest, and surely no other crime but one in the world's history can be paralleled with it.

CHAPTER VII.
THE REHABILITATION.

Twenty years after the events which I have attempted to describe, an act of tardy justice was accorded to Joan of Arc. Charles VII. at length felt it necessary, more for his own interest than for any care of the memory of Joan of Arc, to have a revision made of the iniquitous condemnation of the heroine.

This King, even if unable to rescue the Maid of Orleans from her captors, might at least have attempted her release, yet during all the time--over a year--of her imprisonment he had not even made a sign in her behalf.

There does not exist in the documents of the time a trace of any negotiation, of the smallest offer made to obtain her exchange by prisoners or by ransom, or of any wish to effect her release. But Charles was anxious on his own account, when France had almost wholly been gained back to its allegiance, that his coronation at Rheims should not be imputed to the actions and to the aid of one whom the French clergy and the French judges had condemned and executed as a heretic and apostate. Hence the vast judicial inquiry set on foot by the King to vindicate the fame of her whom the English and the Anglo-French had hoped, through the condemnation pronounced by Cauchon in the name of the Church, to vilify, and through her, by her trial, condemnation, and death, to discredit Charles and his coronation.

On the 15th of February, 1450, Charles VII. declared that Joan of Arc's enemies had destroyed her 'against reason'--so ran the formula--'and very cruelly,' and that it was his, the King's, intention 'to obtain the truth regarding this affair.'

Pope Nicolas V. made difficulties. Cardinal d'Estouteville, who had undertaken to manage the process of rehabilitation, presented the Pope with a claim for a revision of the sentence of condemnation in the name of Joan of Arc's mother and of her two brothers. The petition ran thus: 'The brothers, mother, and relations of Joan, anxious that her memory and their own should be cleansed from this unmerited disgrace, demand that the sentence of condemnation that was given at Rouen shall be annulled.' Not, however, until the death of Pope Nicolas V., and the accession of Calixtus III., was anything further done.

The new Pope (Alfonso Borgia) did not hesitate as to the line he intended taking in the matter, and he gave his sanction to the rehabilitation of the heroine by a rescript dated the 11th of June, 1455. It was as follows:--

'We, Calixtus, servant of the servants of God, accord a favourable ear to the request which has been made us. There has lately been brought before us on the part of Peter and John of Arc, also of Isabella of Arc, their mother, and some of their relations, a petition stating that their sister, daughter, and relative, Joan of Arc deceased, had been unjustly condemned as guilty of the crime of heresy and other crimes against the Faith, on the false testimony of the late William [John, it should be] d'Estivet of the Episcopal Court of Beauvais, and of Peter of happy memory, at that time Bishop of Beauvais, and of the late John Lemaitre, belonging to the Inquisition. The nullity of their proceedings and the innocence of Joan are clearly established both by documents and further by clearest proofs. In consequence of this, the brothers, mother, and relatives of Joan are therefore at liberty to cast off the mark of infamy with which this trial has falsely stamped them; and thus they have humbly supplicated our permission to authorise and to proceed in this trial of rehabilitation.'

The prelates selected by the Pope as commissioners to follow the course of the trial of rehabilitation were John Jouvenel des Ursins, Archbishop of Rheims, William Chartrier, Bishop of Paris, and Richard de Longueil, Bishop of Coutances. On the 7th of November, 1455, this trial was solemnly begun in the Church of Notre Dame, in Paris.

It has been said that Joan of Arc's father died of grief on hearing of his daughter's martyrdom. He was certainly dead before the date of this trial. However, the now aged mother of Joan of Arc, Isabella Romee d'Arc, in her sixty-seventh year, was there. She was supported by her two sons, John and Peter, and was accompanied by many of her relations from Vaucouleurs, and friends from Orleans. The poor soul appears to have been much affected when she appeared before the sympathetic crowd. Many of those present must have come from far to see the mother of the famous heroine claiming at the hands of the Church the vindication of her daughter's fame.

Two meetings took place at Notre Dame, and a third was held at Rouen, at which the family of Joan of Arc were unable to be present--the mother from illness, and the brothers by affairs at home. The ***Procureur***, whose name was Prevosteau, was the advocate for the Arc family. The debates lasted all through the winter, and into the early part of the year 1456. During the debates a hundred articles were drawn up and agreed to, relating to the life, death, and trial of the heroine. None of these are of much importance or interest.

It was not until the witnesses of Joan of Arc's life at home, and of her actions abroad, gave their testimony that the debates became interesting. Then began to pass before the eyes of the spectators a succession of people who had known Joan of Arc, and who had taken part in the same actions as those of the Maid--peasants from her native village, townsfolk from Orleans, generals and soldiers who had ridden with her into battle and fought by her side.

In fact, here appeared all sorts and conditions of men, from farm labourers to princes of the blood royal. The testimony of these people helps one to follow the life of Joan of Arc throughout its short career with something like precision. The sittings of the commissioners took place at Paris, Orleans, Rouen, and also at Domremy. It may be said without exaggeration that the whole of France and all its classes seemed, after an interval of a quarter of a century, to raise its voice in honour of the memory of its martyr Maid, and to attest to the spotless and noble life of her country's saviour.

At Domremy, at Vaucouleurs, and at Toul, thirty-four witnesses were heard on the 28th of January and on the 11th of February, 1456. At Orleans, during the months of February and of March, forty-one depositions were collected by the Archbishop of Rheims.

In Paris, in April and May, the same prelate, assisted by the Bishop of Paris, heard the evidence of twenty witnesses. At Rouen, the same commission heard nineteen others. Finally, at Lyons, the deposition of Joan of Arc's esquire, d'Aulon, who had attended her throughout her campaigns, was made before the Vice-Inquisitor of that province, John Despres.

All these depositions are recorded in Latin, the only exception being that of d'Aulon, which was taken down in French. All those written in Latin have been translated into French by M. Fabre, and published in his ***Proces de Rehabilitation de Jeanne d'Arc***.

Among the witnesses first appear the friends and neighbours of Joan of Arc in her childhood and early years. From her birthplace came her greatest friends, Henriette, Mengette, and Isabellette. The first of these, in the year 1456, was aged forty-five, the second was a year older, and the third was in her fiftieth year. All three were the wives of labourers. Henriette was married to Gerard, Mengette to John Joyart, and Isabellette to Gerardin d'Epinal. To the child of the last Joan had stood god-mother. Next came from the same village three older women, all three being god-mothers to Joan. In those days the French peasantry seem to have had an almost unlimited number of god-fathers and god-mothers. These were named Jeannette, widow of Thepelin de Viteau, aged sixty; Jeannette Theverien, aged sixty-six; and Beatrix, widow of d'Estelin, a labourer of Domremy, then in her eightieth year.

After these three god-mothers, came to give their evidence her god-fathers. Four of these appear--John Rainguesson, John Barrey, John de Langart, and John Morel de Greux. Of these four god-fathers, only the last one seems to have been called to give evidence; he was in his seventieth year. Gerardin d'Epinal, husband of one of the god-mothers, also gave his evidence; it was his son Nicolas for whom Joan of Arc had stood sponsor. In those days it was held that the god-mother of a child stood to it in the relation of a second mother: hence originated the term of 'commere' and 'compere,' which Joan gave the d'Epinals.

Six labourers, who had been playmates with Joan in childhood, then came forward. These men, named respectively Le Cuin, Guillemeth, Waterin, Colin, Masnier, and Jacquard, were between the ages of forty-four and fifty. All these humbly born witnesses agreed in their answers to the twelve questions asked them in the following order:--

1. When and where was Joan born?

2. Who were her parents? Were they of good character and of

good repute?

3. Who were her god-fathers?

4. Was she piously brought up?

5. How did she conduct herself between her seventh year up to the time she left her home?

6. Did she often frequent the churches and places of devotion of her free-will?

7. How did she occupy herself, and what were her duties?

8. Did she confess often?

9. Did she frequent the fairies' tree and the haunted well, and did she go to places with the other young people of the neighbourhood?

10. How did she leave her home, and how did she accomplish her journey?

11. Were any investigations made in her native country at the time she was taken prisoner?

12. Did Joan on one occasion escape to Neufchateau on account of a military raid, and was she then in the company of her parents?

We now arrive at a higher grade in the ranks of the witnesses, in the shape of 'l'honorable homme Nicolas Bailly.' Bailly was a man of sixty; he had been employed by the English in 1430, and by Cauchon--he was a scrivener (tabellion) by profession--to make investigations into the character of Joan in her native place.

Then came the old bell-ringer of Joan of Arc's village--Perrin le Drassier, aged sixty. He told how the maiden loved the sound of the church bells, and how she would blame him when he neglected ringing them, and of her little gifts to him to make him more diligent in his office. After the bell-ringer came three priests--all belonging to the neighbourhood of Domremy. The first--namely, the 'discrete personne Messire Henri Arnolin'--belonged to Gondrecourt-le-Chateau, near to Commercy, and was sixty-four. The next is the 'venerable personne Messire Etienne de Sionne,' curate of the parish church at Raucessey-sous-Neufchateau, aged fifty-four; and the third was named Dominic Jocab, curate of the parish church of Moutier-sur-Saulx.

Next came an old peasant from Domremy, named Bertrand Laclopsse, a thatcher by profession, ninety years of age; after him three neighbours of Joan's father--Thevenin le Royer, seventy years old; Jacquier, sixty; and John Moen, wheelwright, fifty-six. But a far more important witness than any of the preceding three-and-twenty was the uncle of the heroine, Durand Laxart, farm labourer at Burey-le-Petit, whom, it will be remembered, Joan first took into her confidence regarding her voices and her mission. Laxart was then in his sixtieth year. At the close of his evidence he states that all he had said regarding his niece he had also told Charles VII.--probably at the time of the coronation, for Laxart was then at Rheims. Laxart was followed by the couple with whom Joan of Arc lodged when living at Vaucouleurs, Henry and Joan le Royer (or le Charron). After this worthy pair appeared the two brave knights who had guarded the Maid of Orleans during her perilous journey to Chinon--John de Novelem-hont, commonly called John de Metz, aged fifty-seven, and the other, named Bertrand de Poulangy--one of the King's esquires--aged sixty-three.

Three other knights were heard after them--namely, Albert d'Ourche, from Ourche, near Commercy, aged sixty; Geoffrey du Fay, aged fifty; and Louis de Martigny, living at Martigny-les-Gerboneaux, a village near Neufchateau, aged fifty-four. These were followed by two curates and a sergeant. 'Discrete personne Messire Jean le Fumeux,' of Vaucouleurs, canon of the Church of Sainte Marie in that village, also curate of the parish church of d'Ugny, aged only thirty-eight, was, as he admitted, a mere child when Joan of Arc came to Vaucouleurs; but he remembered distinctly having seen her praying in the church at Vaucouleurs, and kneeling for a long time in the subterranean chapel of Sainte Marie's Church before an image of the Blessed Virgin.

The other priest, named John Colin, was the curate of the parish church of Domremy, and a canon of the collegiate church of Saint Nicolas de Brixey, near Vaucouleurs. His age was sixty-six. The last of these thirty-four witnesses was the sergeant, Guillot Jacquier, aged thirty-six: why he was called as a witness does not appear. As a child he had heard Joan of Arc spoken of as 'une brave fille, de bonne renommee, et de conduite honnete,' which opinion was the general one given in their evidence by all the other witnesses, whose names only we have been able to give.

Relating to the period in the life of the heroine between the time of the King's coronation and that of her capture, the facts told by the various persons examined are few and far between. In the trial for the rehabilitation of the Maid of Orleans, the story of her deeds in the field was not of much importance to the commissioners. What they principally desired to ascertain was the fact that no taint of heresy could attach to the life of the heroine. It was for this reason that all those persons who could throw any light upon Joan's early days and the actions of her childhood had been collected to give their evidence. We now come to those witnesses who were examined regarding the life of Joan of Arc after her interview with the King at Chinon and about the stirring events which immediately followed that interview. The first of these is the 'nobile et savant homme Messire Simon Charles,' Master of the Requests (Maitre des requetes) in the year 1429. He had been president of the State exchequer in 1456, and was aged sixty. Simon's evidence is of interest and importance both as regards Joan of Arc's arrival at Chinon, and also with respect to the siege of Orleans and the triumphant entry into Rheims. The next witness was one of the clergy who examined Joan when at Poitiers; this was a preaching friar from Limousin who had asked Joan of Arc in what language her saints spoke to her, and had been answered by 'In a better language than yours'--for this good friar, whose name was Brother Sequier, spoke with a strong Limousin accent. When he was giving his evidence before the commission (in 1456) he was an old man in his seventy-third year, and head of the theological college of Poitiers.

Next to him came the evidence given by the 'venerable et savant homme Maitre Jean Barbier, docteur es lois.' Barbier was King's-Advocate in the House of Parliament, and had also been one of the judges at Joan of Arc's examination at Poitiers: he was aged fifty. Barbier had been at Loches when the people threw themselves before Joan of Arc's horse, and embraced the heroine's feet and hands. Barbier reproved her for allowing them to do so. He told her that if she permitted them to act thus it would render them idolatrous in their worship of her, to which reprimand Joan answered, 'Indeed, without God's help I could not prevent them from becoming so.'

Another of the Poitiers witnesses was Gobert Thibault, also aged fifty. This Thibault had been at Chinon when Joan arrived there, and had followed her to Orleans. Among these Poitiers witnesses was Francis Garivel, aged forty. Garivel, when a lad of fifteen, had seen Joan at Poitiers, and he remembered that on her being asked why she styled Charles Dauphin, and not by his kingly title, she replied that she could not give him his regal title until he had been crowned and anointed at Rheims.

The collected testimony of the above witnesses, whose evidence covers the time passed by Joan at Poitiers, was submitted to Charles VII., and the MSS. exist in the National Library in Paris. It has been edited by the historians Bachon and Quicherat, and translated from the Latin into French by Fabre.

The next batch of witnesses' evidence concerns the fighting period of Joan of Arc's life, and consists principally of the testimony given by her companions in her different campaigns, and this appears to us by far the most interesting and curious.

Of those witnesses the first to testify was a prince of the blood, Joan of Arc's 'beau Duc,' as she loved to call John, Duke of Alencon. He is thus styled in the original document: 'Illustris ac potentissimus princeps et dominus.'

Alencon came of a truly noble line of ancestors, and was descended also from brave warriors. His great-grandfather fell at Crecy, leading the vanguard of the French host. His grandfather was the companion-in-arms of the great Du Guesclin. His father, on the field of Agincourt, after having wounded the Duke of York and stricken him to the ground, crossed swords with King Harry, and then, overwhelmed by numbers, had fallen under a rain of blows.

With Dunois (Bastard of Orleans) Alencon is one of the most prominent of the French leaders who appear in Shakespeare's play, in the first part of ***Henry VI***.

Duke John, like his illustrious forebears, had also fought and bled for his country. His first campaign was made when he was but eighteen. Alencon first saw Joan of Arc in 1429. A strong mutual regard sprang up between the prince and the Maid of Domremy. Alencon had wedded the daughter of the Duke of Orleans, and it was to her that the heroine, when she left with the Duke for their expedition against Paris, promised to bring back her husband in safety.

No one had seen more of Joan of Arc during those days of fighting than had Alencon, and no one bore a higher testimony than did the Duke to her purity, her courage, and the sublime simplicity of her character. It was the Duke of Alencon who was especially struck with the skill shown by the heroine in warlike matters; particularly in her science in the management of artillery--ridiculously rude as that branch of the service appears to us.

'Everybody,' Alencon says, 'was amazed to see that in all that appertained to warfare she acted with as much knowledge and capacity as if she had been twenty or thirty years trained in the art of war.'

Next to Alencon's evidence came that of the famous Bastard of Orleans, the Count de Dunois, one of the most engaging and sympathetic figures of the whole age of chivalry. John of Orleans was the natural son of the Duke of Orleans, and, as Fabre says of him, he 'glorified the appellation of Bastard.' Indeed, the Bastard's name deserves to be handed down in his country's annals with as much glory as that of his great English rival and foe, Talbot, in those of the English. He was a consummate soldier, who even at the early age of twenty-three had brilliantly distinguished himself, and he lived to liberate Normandy and Guyenne from the English.

Well may M. Fabre, in his book on the rehabilitation of Joan of Arc, express his regret that Dunois' evidence was not set forth in the language in which it was delivered, and that it has come down to us weakened by translation into Latin. What is worse is that we have only the translation of a translation.

Dunois had, besides his high military reputation, that of being skilled in oratory. There is, however, in the translation more than a trace of the enthusiasm with which Dunois speaks of the deeds of the heroic maiden. Dunois, Bastard of Orleans as he is always called, bore the following titles, as recited by the chronicler: 'l'illustrieuse prince Jean Comte de Dunois et de Longueville, lieutenant-general de notre seigneur le roi.' He was fifty-one years old in the month of February, 1456.

His deposition extends over the entire period of the life of Joan of Arc between the time of her arrival before Orleans and the period of the King's coronation.

Dunois' evidence closes thus:--'To conclude, it was habitual to Joan to speak playfully on matters relating to war, in order to cheer the soldiers, and she may have alluded to many military events which never were to take place. But I declare that, when she spoke seriously about the war, of her deeds, and of her vocation, she said her work was limited to raising the siege of Orleans, to succouring the unhappy people shut up in that town and in its suburbs, and to leading the King to Rheims for his coronation and anointing.'

Next we have the testimony of the noble knight, Raoul de Gaucourt, who had so stoutly defended Orleans during its long siege. De Gaucourt was eighty-five years old. This fine old warrior's evidence confirms all that Dunois had said in praise of Joan of Arc.

The next to appear was the heroine's page, Louis de Contes, aged fifteen when appointed to attend on Joan of Arc: at the time of the trial of her rehabilitation he was forty-two.

Next came a very interesting witness, to wit, Joan of Arc's almoner, 'venerable et religieux personne Jean Pasquerel.' This worthy priest had been formerly in a Tours monastery. We do not find his age given at this time. The clear graphic testimony of this good man is a pleasure to read. His love and admiration for the heroine appear in every line of his testimony, and although this narrative is already too long, it will not perhaps be considered tedious if some of his evidence is quoted.

'When I first had tidings,' he says, 'of Joan of Arc and of her arrival at Court, I was at Puy, where at that time were her mother and some people who had accompanied her to Chinon. Having come to me, they said, "You must come with us and see Joan; we will not allow you to leave us until you have seen her." So I went with them to Chinon, and also to Tours. At that time I was reader in a convent in that town. When she came to Tours, Joan lived in the house of John Dupuy, a burgher of that place. It was there that I first met her. "Joan," they said to her, "we have brought this good father to see you. When you know him well you will like him very much." And Joan answered them and said, "The good father pleases me much; I have heard about him already, and I will make my confession to him tomorrow."

'And I heard her confession on the day following, when I also sang the Mass before her. Since that I have always followed Joan, and I remained her chaplain till the time of her capture at Compiegne.'

It was in this good priest's evidence that the touching trait of Joan of Arc's fondness for gathering children about her was made known. 'She confessed nearly every day,' he said, 'and took the Sacrament often. When near any community of begging friars she asked me to remind her of the days on which the beggar children received the Eucharist, so that she might receive it at the same time with them. It was her delight,' he said, 'to take the Sacrament along with the poor mendicant children. She shed tears often at confession.'

Later on in his evidence Pasquerel adds to the above, 'that often at night I have seen her kneeling, praying for her King and for the success of her mission. I certainly,' he said, 'firmly believed in the divine source of her mission, for she was always engaged in good works, and she was full of every good quality. During a campaign when provisions ran short Joan would never take that which had been gained by pillage. To the wounded she was ever pitiful--to the English as well as to those of her own country, and she always tried to get them to make their confession, if badly, and even if only slightly, wounded. The fear of God was ever before her, nor would she for anything in the world do anything which she considered contrary to His will: for instance, when she was wounded in the shoulder by the dart from a crossbow, when some people wished her to allow the wound to be charmed, promising that if she had it done her hurt would be healed, Joan said that to do so would be a sin, and that she would sooner die than commit one.

'I am greatly surprised,' continued the unsophisticated old priest, 'that such great lawyers (grands clercs) as were those at Rouen could have sentenced Joan to death. How could they put to death that poor child, who was such a good and such a simple Christian, and that too, so cruelly, without a reason--for surely they had not sufficient reason at any rate to kill her!'

Pasquerel could evidently not grasp the real reason for the part played by Cauchon in the execution of the Maid of Orleans, or imagine that in order to obtain an archbishopric his beloved Joan had been condemned by the Bishop of Beauvais to the flames. Pasquerel's evidence ends thus:--

'I have nothing more to add except this. On several occasions Joan told me that if she were to die, she hoped our lord the King would found chantries in which the Almighty might be entreated in intercession for the souls of those who had been slain in the defence of the kingdom.'

The next witness is John d'Aulon, knight, Seneschal of Beaucaire, member of the King's Council. It was he who had served Joan of Arc as esquire during all her campaigns. His evidence is of importance, as it proves clearly the grounds on which the trial of rehabilitation was held--namely, to clear the King of having been crowned and anointed through the agency of one condemned by the Church as an apostate and heretic. The Archbishop thus wrote to d'Aulon on the 20th of April, 1456:--

'By the sentence pronounced against Joan the English wish it to be believed that the Maid was a sorceress, a heretic, and in league with the devil, and therefore that the King had received his kingdom by those means; and thus they hold as heretics the King and those that have served him.'

Nothing can be clearer than this declaration, or show better the real object for which that utterly selfish prince, Charles VII., had, after the lapse of a quarter of a century since the death of Joan of Arc, instituted these proceedings--not at all in order to do honour to the heroine's memory, but in order that his position as King of France should not be tainted with the heresy which had been charged to the account of Joan by and through the clergy and French doctors of theology and learning.

D'Aulon's evidence is one of the most complete of the entire set of testimonies. It was given, not at Rouen, but at Lyons, in 1456, before the Vice-Inquisitor, John Despres.

His depositions are remarkable in this, that, unlike those of the other witnesses, they are recorded in French, and not in Latin.

Next to d'Aulon succeeds, in the chain of witnesses, Simon Beaucroix, aged fifty. Simon was a youth at Chinon when Joan of Arc came there. Beaucroix's evidence is followed by that of John Luillier, a citizen of Orleans. He bore evidence to the immense popularity of the Maid during and after the siege of Orleans. At the time of the trial of rehabilitation Luillier was fifty. To the part played by the Maid at the siege of his native town he speaks thus:--

'As to the question you put me, whether I think the siege of Orleans was raised and the town saved from the enemy by the intervention and the ministration (ministere) of the Maid, even more than by the force of arms, this is my answer: All my fellow citizens, as well as I myself, believe that had the Maid not come there by the will of God to our rescue, we should very soon, both town and people, have been in the power of the besiegers. It is my belief,' he adds, 'that it was impossible for the people of Orleans and for the army present at Orleans to have held out much longer against the superior strength of the enemy.'

More people from Orleans next gave their evidence: viz. William le Charron, John Volant, William Postian, Denis Roger, James de Thou, John Canelier, Aignan de Saint-Mesmin, John Hilaire, Jacques l'Esbalny, Cosme de Commy, John de Champcoux, Peter Hue, Peter Jonqualt, John Aubert, William Rouillart, Gentien Cabu, Peter Vaillant, John Beaucharnys, John Coulon. All these men were burghers of the town, and their ages varied between forty and seventy. All agreed with Luillier in their belief that, under God, it was Joan of Arc who rescued their city from the English.

Following these men we now come to the evidence of some of the women who had seen or known the heroine. First of these is Joan, wife of Gilles de Saint-Mesmin, aged seventy. She says: 'The general opinion was and is still at Orleans that Joan was a good Catholic--simple, humble, and of a holy life.' Such, too, is the opinion of Joan, the wife of Guy Boyleau, and of Guillemette, wife of John de Coulon; also of the widow of John de Mouchy. All these agree with the first lady's testimony.

We have next the evidence of the daughter of James Boucher, the treasurer of Orleans, at whose house Joan of Arc lodged while in Orleans. Charlotte Boucher had married William Houet. When her deposition was taken in 1456 she was thirty-six years old, and consequently only nine when Joan lodged at her father's house. However, young as she was then, the visit of the Maid had left a great memory behind; she had been Joan's bed-fellow.

'Often,' she says, 'Joan said to my mother, "Hope in God, for He will deliver the town of Orleans, and drive the enemy away."'

And last we find the evidence of two good wives of Orleans, one widow of John Hure, the other Petronille, wife of Beaucharnys. After these came six clerics, canons of the Church of Saint Aignan at Orleans--Robert de Farciaux, Peter Compaing,

Peter de la Censurey, Raoul Godert, Herve Bonart, and Andre Bordez. Peter Milet and his wife, Colette, were also witnesses. All had known Joan when she was at Orleans, as had Aignan Viole, an advocate of Parliament, who had been in Orleans during the siege.

The 'noble homme Guillaume de Richarville, panetier de la cour,' gave his evidence, relating to Joan of Arc's appearance at Court, as also did an old Court physician named Reginald Thierry; it is he who relates how, at the capture of Saint Pierre-le-Moutier, Joan prevented its church from being pillaged.

A doughty warrior follows, namely, 'noble et prudent Seigneur le chevalier Thibauld d'Armagnac, Sire de Thermes, Bailli de Chartres.' D'Armagnac was fifty years old; he had followed Joan of Arc all through her campaign, and, like Alencon, had a very high opinion of her military talents. At the close of his evidence, he says: 'In the manner of the conduct and ordering of troops, in that of placing them in battle array, and of animating the men, Joan of Arc had as much capacity for these things as the most accomplished captain in the art of war.'

After the soldier, the peasant. This peasant, or rather mechanic, is a coppersmith named Husson Lemaitre. Lemaitre hailed from Domremy. Being in the year 1456 at Rouen, he then and there gave his evidence. He had known Joan of Arc's family, and Joan too in her childhood; of all of them he spoke most highly.

Next comes 'honnete et prude femme demoiselle Marguerite la Tournelle,' the widow of Rene de Bouligny. It was at her house at Bourges that Joan lodged after the coronation at Rheims.

We now pass to an entirely different category of witnesses. These are the men who sat in the trial of the heroine. One can well understand the embarrassment shown by such folk in their replies to the questions they had to answer, and their wish if it were possible to turn the responsibility of their previous judgment on the heads of those who were no longer in this world to answer the charges made against them.

The first of these men is 'venerable et savante personne Maitre Thomas de Courcelles.' De Courcelles was only fifty-six in 1456, when called on to make his deposition as to the part he had played in the heroine's trial at Rouen, five-and-twenty years before. His evidence is full of the feeblest argument, and his memory appears to have been a very convenient one, as he repeatedly evades an answer by the plea of having forgotten all about the incident alluded to.

Next follows that 'venerable et circonspecte personne, Maitre Jean Beaupere'--a doctor of theology, and canon of Rouen, Paris, and Besancon. This circumspect person was now in his seventieth year. He laid most of the blame of Joan of Arc's death upon the English, and the rest on Cauchon. The English being away, and Cauchon dead, the circumspection of this doctor's evidence is evident.

We next have that of the Bishop of Noyon, John de Mailly. This bishop had been in the service of the English King, but had, when Charles became prosperous, returned to him. In 1456 he was aged sixty. An intimate of the Prince Cardinal of Winchester, and one of the foremost of the judges who condemned Joan of Arc to death, his deposition in 1456 is quite a study in the art of trying to convince people that black is white. He had shown some kind of feeling of humanity at the time of the martyrdom of the Maid, and had left that scene of horror early. To the memory of his old friend and colleague, Cauchon, he gives a parting kick by saying at the close of his examination that of one thing he was quite certain, and that was that Cauchon received money for the conduct of the trial from his friends, the English. But he might have now been reminded that he too had received some of this blood-money.

Next to appear is another French bishop, Monseigneur Jean Le Fevre, Eveque in partibus de Demetriade. This prelate was in his seventieth year. At the time of Joan of Arc's trial he was professor of theology of the order of hermit monks of Saint Augustins. The Bishop had taken an active part in the trial and condemnation. Like his brother bishop, Le Fevre enjoyed a very convenient memory, and had quite forgotten many things of importance which occurred during the trial in 1430. Nor did he even take part as a spectator in the martyrdom which he had helped to bring about--'I left before the end,' he said, 'not feeling the strength to see more.' Let that shred of humanity in the composition of priests like him be allowed before we entirely condemn them.

The next witness is also a Churchman, Peter Migiet, the prior of Longueville, aged seventy. He also had been one of Cauchon's crawling creatures. There is little of interest in his evidence, except the passage where he says that an English knight had told him that the English feared Joan of Arc more than a hundred soldiers, and that her very name was a source of terror to the foe. Although this sounds an exaggerated statement, it is not so, as is proved by an edict having been issued by the English Government in the May of 1430, in which English officers and soldiers who refused to enter France for fear of 'the enchantments of the Maid' were threatened with severe punishment. There is, moreover, an edict, bearing the date of December 1430, which was also issued by the English military authorities, describing the trial and the punishment by court martial of all soldiers who had deserted the army in France from fear of Joan of Arc.

After the above priests, on whom rests the infamy of having taken part in the death of the heroine, it is a relief to find the next witness, although a Churchman, a man of sufficient honesty and courage to have been one of those few who refused to take any part in the iniquitous proceedings connected with Joan of Arc's trial, and who suffered imprisonment owing to his unwillingness to carry out Cauchon's wishes. This worthy priest was named Nicolas de Houppeville, a doctor of theology, now in his sixty-fifth year.

The next witness is John Tiphanie, a canon of the Sainte Chapelle of Paris. He was also a doctor in medicine. Tiphanie had been compelled much against his inclination to take part in the trial of Joan. He was one of the doctors who were sent to see her when she lay ill in prison.

Then follows another doctor; this is William Delachambre, aged only forty-eight in 1456. He must have practised his vocation at a very early age. Delachambre had also joined in the trial of the Maid, from fear of Cauchon. His evidence relating to the scene at Saint Ouen is important.

'I remember well,' he says, 'the abjuration which Joan of Arc made. She hesitated a long while before she made it. At length William Erard determined her to make it by telling her that, when she had made it, she should be delivered from her prison. Under this promise she at length decided to do so, and she then read a short profession of some six or seven lines written on a piece of folded paper. I was so near that I could see the writing on the paper.'

We next come to the witness whose evidence is, next to that of Dunois, of the greatest importance; it is that of the Recorder, or judges' clerk, William Manchon. Born in 1395, he was sixty-one years of age when the rehabilitation trial took place. Manchon's evidence takes up thirty pages in M. Fabre's work, already often referred to--Le Proces de Rehabilitation de Jeanne d'Arc. Much against his will was

Manchon obliged to act in the trial of the Maid, but he did not dare disobey the orders of those who formed the Council of Henry VI. All that he deposed has been made use of in the account of the heroine's life; so now we need do no more than refer to it. The other Recorder who helped Manchon to draw up the minutes of the trial was also examined; this was William Colles, called Boisguillaume. He was in his sixty-sixth year. Colles relates that, after the execution, the people used to point out the author of Joan's death with horror--'besides,' he adds, 'I have been told that the most prominent of those who took part in her condemnation died miserably. Nicolas Midi [who had preached the sermon on the day of her execution, and just before it took place] was stricken with leprosy, and Cauchon died suddenly, while being shaved.'

A third Recorder was also examined, Nicolas Taquel. Then followed the priest Massieu. During the trial of Joan he had acted as bailiff to the Court, and in that capacity had seen much of the prisoner; he had always conveyed her to and from her prison. It may be remembered that it was he who, on Joan's petition to be allowed to kneel before the chapel on her way to the hall of judgment, granted her request, and was threatened by Cauchon, should it again occur, to be thrown into prison where, as Cauchon said to him, he would not have 'the light of sun or moon.' Massieu remained till the end with Joan, and it is he who records that the executioner found, after the body had been destroyed, that the heart remained unconsumed. He also relates that the executioner was ordered to collect the ashes and all that remained, and to throw those few relics of humanity into the Seine, which was accordingly done. Martin Ladvenu followed Massieu. Ladvenu was a Dominican friar: he was one of the few priests who showed some humanity to the victim. It was to him that Joan of Arc confessed on the morning of her death, and it was also to him that the executioner came on the night of the martyrdom, and said that no execution had ever affected him as that one had done. Next to arrive was Isambard de la Pierre, a Dominican priest. He had been an acolyte of the Vice-Inquisitor, Lemaitre; he too, like Ladvenu, had shown sympathy with the sufferer, had given her advice during the trial, and had helped to soothe her last moments. De la Pierre states in his evidence regarding her supposed refusal to submit herself to the Church, that Joan of Arc, when she was told by her judges to submit herself, thought they meant themselves by the Church of which they spoke to her; but when she was told by him what the Church really signified she always said she submitted herself to it and to the Pope. It was to Isambard de la Pierre that Joan begged for a cross when on the pile and about to die. 'As I was close by the poor child,' he says, 'she begged me humbly to go to the church close at hand and bring her a cross to hold up right before her eyes, till her death, so that the cross on which God hung might as long as she lived appear before her. She died a true and good Christian. In the midst of the flames she never ceased calling on the sacred name of Jesus, and invoking the aid of the saints in Paradise. When the fire was lit she begged me to get down from off the stake with my cross, but to hold it still before her, which I did. At last, bending down her head, with a strong voice calling on the name of Jesus, she gave up the ghost.'

Yet another priest succeeds: this is 'venerable et religieux personne, frere Jean Toutmouille,' of the order of the preaching friars of Rouen. Toutmouille was quite a youth at the time of Joan of Arc's death. Another priest follows, William Daval, also one of the order of preaching friars, and belonging to the Church of Saint James at Rouen. He, too, had been, with Isambard, one of the acolytes of the Vice-Inquisitor. In his evidence, he tells of how, after Isambard had been advising Joan in her prison, he was met by Warwick, who threatened to have him thrown into the river if he continued seeing the prisoner.

We next have 'venerable et circonspecte personne Maitre Andre Marguerie'; this was one of Cauchon's most trusted creatures. His 'ame damnee,' Richard de Grouchet, canon of the collegiate Church of Sans Faye, is the next witness. There is nothing of any interest in the testimony of these Churchmen, nor in that of Nicolas Dubesert, another canon of Rouen, nor in that of Nicolas Caval. Next appears a prior, Thomas Marie, of the Church of Saint Michel, near Rouen. Four other ecclesiastics follow them--John Roquier, Peter Bouchier, John Bonnet, John de Lenozoles; but none of these men's testimony is of any interest. The evidence of no less a person than the torturer is called next. He is named--to give him his titles in full--'Honnete homme Mauger Lessarmentrer, clerc non marier, appariteur de la cour archiepiscopalle de Rouen.' The name of the chief torturer of the good city of Rouen, Mauger, has a gruesome ring about it--it reminds one of the headsman in Harrison Ainsworth's novel of the ***Tower of London***. Aged fifty-six in 1456, Mauger had seen Joan of Arc when she was brought into the yet extant tower of the castle, and threatened by Cauchon with the torture. 'We were,' deposed Mauger, 'my companion and myself, ordered to go there to torture her. She was questioned, and she answered with much prudence, and so well, that every one was amazed. Finally, I and my companion left the tower without having laid hands upon her.' Mauger attended at the execution, and this is what he heard and saw there and then. 'As soon as the Bishop (Cauchon) had read the sentence, Joan was taken to the fire. I did not hear whether the civil judges delivered the sentence or not. Joan was placed instantly upon the fire. In the midst of the flames she called out more than six times the name of Jesus. It was when about to give the last breath that she called out with a loud voice, "Jesus!" so that every one could hear her. Nearly everybody wept, for all were overcome with pity.'

After the torturer's witness came that of a soldier, Aimonde de Macy, who was thirty years old when he met Joan in the Castle of Beaurevoir; she being then a prisoner in the charge of Ligny.

De Macy was at Rouen at the time when Lord Stafford came so nearly stabbing the Maid in her prison, and was only prevented from that dastardly act by Warwick.

We next hear the evidence of an attorney, Peter Daron: he had also seen Joan in her prison at Rouen, and had seen her die.

Next we have 'prudent homme Maitre Jean Fave, maitre des requetes du roi Charles VII.': he, too, was present at the execution.

Next appears upon the scene 'honnete personne Laurent Guesdon,' clerk and advocate to the lay court of Rouen. He also had been present at the death of Joan of Arc, and, from his office as lieutenant of the Bailiff of Rouen, he held an important position at the execution; and this is some of his evidence relating to it: 'I assisted at the last sermon preached at the old market-place. I had accompanied the Bailiff, being then his deputy. The sentence was read by which Joan was abandoned to the secular arm; after that sentence had been pronounced the executioners seized her, before either the Bailiff or myself had time to read the sentence; and she was led up to the stake--which was not as it should have been ordered.'

Next arrive as witnesses two burghers of Rouen, Peter Cusquel and John Moreaux. Both of them had been spectators of the martyrdom, but they have nothing of interest to say about it. And finally--(and doubtless the reader will be glad to come to the end of this interminable procession, as is the writer)--comes the deposition of John Marcel--'bourgeois' of Paris. Marcel had been in Rouen during the time of the Maid's trial, and was also present at the end of her life. M. Fabre, in concluding in his book the translation of the testimonies of the long list of witnesses given by him for the first time in full, makes a great point of the universal concurrence of those who knew Joan of Arc as to her undoubted purity of person as well as of mind: that fact is of the greatest importance as regarded the rehabilitation of the Maid of Orleans. That is a subject which it is not now necessary to do more than to allude to; but to the French judges in the time of the trial of the rehabilitation, the fact of Joan of Arc being proved to have been incontestably a virgin was of the highest interest. It was reserved for a countryman of Joan of Arc's (Du Bellay) to invent a legend to disprove the fact; and to the everlasting shame of French literature, Voltaire adopted the lying calumny in his licentious burlesque-heroic poem, ***La Pucelle d'Orleans***.

The sentence of rehabilitation which fills in the translation a dozen of M. Fabre's pages, was solemnly delivered in the great hall of the archiepiscopal palace at Rouen. On that occasion one of Joan of Arc's brothers, John, was present. The sentence which was framed to wipe away the iniquity of the judgment by which the heroine had been condemned, was delivered by the Archbishop of Rheims in the presence of a vast concourse of people, among whom were the Bishops of Paris and of Coutances. Among other things ordered to honour the memory of the Martyr, it was ordained that after a sermon preached on the spot where the act of abjuration had taken place in the cemetery of the Church of Saint Ouen, and also on the site of the spot where had stood the stake and pyre, two crosses should be erected.

Crosses were placed not only there, and in Rouen, but also on other spots. It is interesting to know that one of these crosses can still be seen in the Forest of Compiegne; and it is traditionally said that this cross at Compiegne was placed there by no other than Dunois himself. Both the crosses at Rouen have disappeared centuries ago. Processions took place at Rouen, and all was done that the Church could do to wash out the indelible stain of its action four-and-twenty years before the time of the rehabilitation. In 1431, the clergy of France, to please the English, had in the name of orthodoxy, and with the tolerance of the Pope, denounced Joan of Arc as 'a heretic and idolatress.' In 1456, the same French clergy, to please Charles VII., in the name of religion and justice pronounced the memory of Joan of Arc free from all taint of heresy and of idolatry, and ordered processions and erected crosses in her honour to keep her memory fresh in the land.

www.bookjungle.com *email: sales@bookjungle.com fax: 630-214-0564 mail: Book Jungle PO Box 2226 Champaign, IL 61825*

The Codes Of Hammurabi And Moses
W. W. Davies

QTY

The discovery of the Hammurabi Code is one of the greatest achievements of archaeology, and is of paramount interest, not only to the student of the Bible, but also to all those interested in ancient history...

Religion   **ISBN:** *1-59462-338-4*   Pages:132
MSRP *$12.95*

The Theory of Moral Sentiments
Adam Smith

QTY

This work from 1749. contains original theories of conscience amd moral judgment and it is the foundation for systemof morals.

Philosophy   **ISBN:** *1-59462-777-0*   Pages:536
MSRP *$19.95*

Jessica's First Prayer
Hesba Stretton

QTY

In a screened and secluded corner of one of the many railway-bridges which span the streets of London there could be seen a few years ago, from five o'clock every morning until half past eight, a tidily set-out coffee-stall, consisting of a trestle and board, upon which stood two large tin cans, with a small fire of charcoal burning under each so as to keep the coffee boiling during the early hours of the morning when the work-people were thronging into the city on their way to their daily toil...

Childrens   **ISBN:** *1-59462-373-2*   Pages:84
MSRP *$9.95*

My Life and Work
Henry Ford

QTY

Henry Ford revolutionized the world with his implementation of mass production for the Model T automobile. Gain valuable business insight into his life and work with his own auto-biography... "We have only started on our development of our country we have not as yet, with all our talk of wonderful progress, done more than scratch the surface. The progress has been wonderful enough but..."

Biographies/   **ISBN:** *1-59462-198-5*   Pages:300
MSRP *$21.95*

www.bookjungle.com *email: sales@bookjungle.com fax: 630-214-0564 mail: Book Jungle PO Box 2226 Champaign, IL 61825*

The Art of Cross-Examination
Francis Wellman

QTY

I presume it is the experience of every author, after his first book is published upon an important subject, to be almost overwhelmed with a wealth of ideas and illustrations which could readily have been included in his book, and which to his own mind, at least, seem to make a second edition inevitable. Such certainly was the case with me; and when the first edition had reached its sixth impression in five months, I rejoiced to learn that it seemed to my publishers that the book had met with a sufficiently favorable reception to justify a second and considerably enlarged edition. ...

Reference   ISBN: *1-59462-647-2*   **Pages:412**   *MSRP $19.95*

On the Duty of Civil Disobedience
Henry David Thoreau

QTY

Thoreau wrote his famous essay, On the Duty of Civil Disobedience, as a protest against an unjust but popular war and the immoral but popular institution of slave-owning. He did more than write—he declined to pay his taxes, and was hauled off to gaol in consequence. Who can say how much this refusal of his hastened the end of the war and of slavery ?

Law   ISBN: *1-59462-747-9*   **Pages:48**   *MSRP $7.45*

Dream Psychology Psychoanalysis for Beginners
Sigmund Freud

QTY

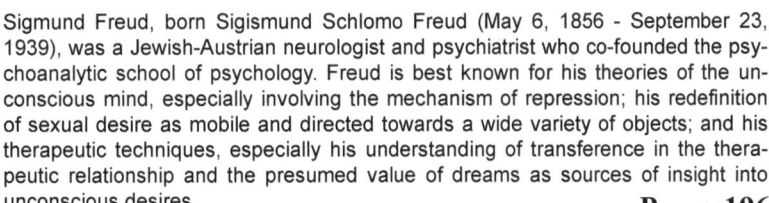

Sigmund Freud, born Sigismund Schlomo Freud (May 6, 1856 - September 23, 1939), was a Jewish-Austrian neurologist and psychiatrist who co-founded the psychoanalytic school of psychology. Freud is best known for his theories of the unconscious mind, especially involving the mechanism of repression; his redefinition of sexual desire as mobile and directed towards a wide variety of objects; and his therapeutic techniques, especially his understanding of transference in the therapeutic relationship and the presumed value of dreams as sources of insight into unconscious desires.

Psychology   ISBN: *1-59462-905-6*   **Pages:196**   *MSRP $15.45*

The Miracle of Right Thought
Orison Swett Marden

QTY

Believe with all of your heart that you will do what you were made to do. When the mind has once formed the habit of holding cheerful, happy, prosperous pictures, it will not be easy to form the opposite habit. It does not matter how improbable or how far away this realization may see, or how dark the prospects may be, if we visualize them as best we can, as vividly as possible, hold tenaciously to them and vigorously struggle to attain them, they will gradually become actualized, realized in the life. But a desire, a longing without endeavor, a yearning abandoned or held indifferently will vanish without realization.

Self Help   ISBN: *1-59462-644-8*   **Pages:360**   *MSRP $25.45*

www.bookjungle.com email: sales@bookjungle.com fax: 630-214-0564 mail: Book Jungle PO Box 2226 Champaign, IL 61825

QTY

	Title	ISBN	Price
☐	**The Rosicrucian Cosmo-Conception Mystic Christianity** by *Max Heindel*	ISBN: 1-59462-188-8	$38.95
	The Rosicrucian Cosmo-conception is not dogmatic, neither does it appeal to any other authority than the reason of the student. It is: not controversial, but is: sent forth in the, hope that it may help to clear...	New Age/Religion Pages 646	
☐	**Abandonment To Divine Providence** by *Jean-Pierre de Caussade*	ISBN: 1-59462-228-0	$25.95
	"The Rev. Jean Pierre de Caussade was one of the most remarkable spiritual writers of the Society of Jesus in France in the 18th Century. His death took place at Toulouse in 1751. His works have gone through many editions and have been republished...	Inspirational/Religion Pages 400	
☐	**Mental Chemistry** by *Charles Haanel*	ISBN: 1-59462-192-6	$23.95
	Mental Chemistry allows the change of material conditions by combining and appropriately utilizing the power of the mind. Much like applied chemistry creates something new and unique out of careful combinations of chemicals the mastery of mental chemistry...	New Age Pages 354	
☐	**The Letters of Robert Browning and Elizabeth Barret Barrett 1845-1846 vol II** by *Robert Browning* and *Elizabeth Barrett*	ISBN: 1-59462-193-4	$35.95
		Biographies Pages 596	
☐	**Gleanings In Genesis (volume I)** by *Arthur W. Pink*	ISBN: 1-59462-130-6	$27.45
	Appropriately has Genesis been termed "the seed plot of the Bible" for in it we have, in germ form, almost all of the great doctrines which are afterwards fully developed in the books of Scripture which follow...	Religion/Inspirational Pages 420	
☐	**The Master Key** by *L. W. de Laurence*	ISBN: 1-59462-001-6	$30.95
	In no branch of human knowledge has there been a more lively increase of the spirit of research during the past few years than in the study of Psychology, Concentration and Mental Discipline. The requests for authentic lessons in Thought Control, Mental Discipline and...	New Age/Business Pages 422	
☐	**The Lesser Key Of Solomon Goetia** by *L. W. de Laurence*	ISBN: 1-59462-092-X	$9.95
	This translation of the first book of the "Lernegton" which is now for the first time made accessible to students of Talismanic Magic was done, after careful collation and edition, from numerous Ancient Manuscripts in Hebrew, Latin, and French...	New Age/Occult Pages 92	
☐	**Rubaiyat Of Omar Khayyam** by *Edward Fitzgerald*	ISBN: 1-59462-332-5	$13.95
	Edward Fitzgerald, whom the world has already learned, in spite of his own efforts to remain within the shadow of anonymity, to look upon as one of the rarest poets of the century, was born at Bredfield, in Suffolk, on the 31st of March, 1809. He was the third son of John Purcell...	Music Pages 172	
☐	**Ancient Law** by *Henry Maine*	ISBN: 1-59462-128-4	$29.95
	The chief object of the following pages is to indicate some of the earliest ideas of mankind, as they are reflected in Ancient Law, and to point out the relation of those ideas to modern thought.	Religiom/History Pages 452	
☐	**Far-Away Stories** by *William J. Locke*	ISBN: 1-59462-129-2	$19.45
	"Good wine needs no bush, but a collection of mixed vintages does. And this book is just such a collection. Some of the stories I do not want to remain buried for ever in the museum files of dead magazine-numbers an author's not unpardonable vanity..."	Fiction Pages 272	
☐	**Life of David Crockett** by *David Crockett*	ISBN: 1-59462-250-7	$27.45
	"Colonel David Crockett was one of the most remarkable men of the times in which he lived. Born in humble life, but gifted with a strong will, an indomitable courage, and unremitting perseverance...	Biographies/New Age Pages 424	
☐	**Lip-Reading** by *Edward Nitchie*	ISBN: 1-59462-206-X	$25.95
	Edward B. Nitchie, founder of the New York School for the Hard of Hearing, now the Nitchie School of Lip-Reading, Inc, wrote "LIP-READING Principles and Practice". The development and perfecting of this meritorious work on lip-reading was an undertaking...	How-to Pages 400	
☐	**A Handbook of Suggestive Therapeutics, Applied Hypnotism, Psychic Science** by *Henry Munro*	ISBN: 1-59462-214-0	$24.95
		Health/New Age/Health/Self-help Pages 376	
☐	**A Doll's House: and Two Other Plays** by *Henrik Ibsen*	ISBN: 1-59462-112-8	$19.95
	Henrik Ibsen created this classic when in revolutionary 1848 Rome. Introducing some striking concepts in playwriting for the realist genre, this play has been studied the world over.	Fiction/Classics/Plays 308	
☐	**The Light of Asia** by *sir Edwin Arnold*	ISBN: 1-59462-204-3	$13.95
	In this poetic masterpiece, Edwin Arnold describes the life and teachings of Buddha. The man who was to become known as Buddha to the world was born as Prince Gautama of India but he rejected the worldly riches and abandoned the reigns of power when...	Religion/History/Biographies Pages 170	
☐	**The Complete Works of Guy de Maupassant** by *Guy de Maupassant*	ISBN: 1-59462-157-8	$16.95
	"For days and days, nights and nights, I had dreamed of that first kiss which was to consecrate our engagement, and I knew not on what spot I should put my lips..."	Fiction/Classics Pages 240	
☐	**The Art of Cross-Examination** by *Francis L. Wellman*	ISBN: 1-59462-309-0	$26.95
	Written by a renowned trial lawyer, Wellman imparts his experience and uses case studies to explain how to use psychology to extract desired information through questioning.	How-to/Science/Reference Pages 408	
☐	**Answered or Unanswered?** by *Louisa Vaughan* Miracles of Faith in China	ISBN: 1-59462-248-5	$10.95
		Religion Pages 112	
☐	**The Edinburgh Lectures on Mental Science (1909)** by *Thomas*	ISBN: 1-59462-008-3	$11.95
	This book contains the substance of a course of lectures recently given by the writer in the Queen Street Hall, Edinburgh. Its purpose is to indicate the Natural Principles governing the relation between Mental Action and Material Conditions...	New Age/Psychology Pages 148	
☐	**Ayesha** by *H. Rider Haggard*	ISBN: 1-59462-301-5	$24.95
	Verily and indeed it is the unexpected that happens! Probably if there was one person upon the earth from whom the Editor of this, and of a certain previous history, did not expect to hear again...	Classics Pages 380	
☐	**Ayala's Angel** by *Anthony Trollope*	ISBN: 1-59462-352-X	$29.95
	The two girls were both pretty, but Lucy who was twenty-one who supposed to be simple and comparatively unattractive, whereas Ayala was credited, as her Bombwhat romantic name might show, with poetic charm and a taste for romance. Ayala when her father died was nineteen...	Fiction Pages 484	
☐	**The American Commonwealth** by *James Bryce*	ISBN: 1-59462-286-8	$34.45
	An interpretation of American democratic political theory. It examines political mechanics and society from the perspective of Scotsman James Bryce	Politics Pages 572	
☐	**Stories of the Pilgrims** by *Margaret P. Pumphrey*	ISBN: 1-59462-116-0	$17.95
	This book explores pilgrims religious oppression in England as well as their escape to Holland and eventual crossing to America on the Mayflower, and their early days in New England...	History Pages 268	

www.bookjungle.com *email: sales@bookjungle.com fax: 630-214-0564 mail: Book Jungle PO Box 2226 Champaign, IL 61825*

QTY

The Fasting Cure *by Sinclair Upton* ISBN: *1-59462-222-1* **$13.95**
In the Cosmopolitan Magazine for May, 1910, and in the Contemporary Review (London) for April, 1910, I published an article dealing with my experiences in fasting. I have written a great many magazine articles, but never one which attracted so much attention... *New Age/Self Help/Health Pages 164*

Hebrew Astrology *by Sepharial* ISBN: *1-59462-308-2* **$13.45**
In these days of advanced thinking it is a matter of common observation that we have left many of the old landmarks behind and that we are now pressing forward to greater heights and to a wider horizon than that which represented the mind-content of our progenitors... *Astrology Pages 144*

Thought Vibration or The Law of Attraction in the Thought World ISBN: *1-59462-127-6* **$12.95**
by William Walker Atkinson *Psychology/Religion Pages 144*

Optimism *by Helen Keller* ISBN: *1-59462-108-X* **$15.95**
Helen Keller was blind, deaf, and mute since 19 months old, yet famously learned how to overcome these handicaps, communicate with the world, and spread her lectures promoting optimism. An inspiring read for everyone... *Biographies/Inspirational Pages 84*

Sara Crewe *by Frances Burnett* ISBN: *1-59462-360-0* **$9.45**
In the first place, Miss Minchin lived in London. Her home was a large, dull, tall one, in a large, dull square, where all the houses were alike, and all the sparrows were alike, and where all the door-knockers made the same heavy sound... *Childrens/Classic Pages 88*

The Autobiography of Benjamin Franklin *by Benjamin Franklin* ISBN: *1-59462-135-7* **$24.95**
The Autobiography of Benjamin Franklin has probably been more extensively read than any other American historical work, and no other book of its kind has had such ups and downs of fortune. Franklin lived for many years in England, where he was agent... *Biographies/History Pages 332*

Name	
Email	
Telephone	
Address	
City, State ZIP	

☐ Credit Card   ☐ Check / Money Order

Credit Card Number	
Expiration Date	
Signature	

Please Mail to: Book Jungle
PO Box 2226
Champaign, IL 61825
or Fax to: 630-214-0564

ORDERING INFORMATION

web: *www.bookjungle.com*
email: *sales@bookjungle.com*
fax: *630-214-0564*
mail: *Book Jungle PO Box 2226 Champaign, IL 61825*
or PayPal *to sales@bookjungle.com*

Please contact us for bulk discounts

DIRECT-ORDER TERMS

**20% Discount if You Order
Two or More Books**
Free Domestic Shipping!
Accepted: Master Card, Visa,
Discover, American Express

www.ingramcontent.com/pod-product-compliance
Lightning Source LLC
Chambersburg PA
CBHW081232170426
43198CB00017B/2731